MW01051254

# MONEY MUSIC 101

## ESSENTIAL FINANCE SKILLS

### for musicians, artists & creative entrepreneurs

# CLEMENS KOWNATZKI

Copyright © 2011 Clemens Kownatzki
All rights reserved.

**Disclaimer**
The publisher and author have used their best efforts in preparing this book but make no representation with regard to the accuracy and completeness of the contents provided. Neither the information nor any opinion contained in this book constitutes a solicitation or offer to buy or to sell any securities, futures, options or other financial instruments or to provide any investment advice or service. Each decision by you to do any investment transactions and each decision whether a particular investment is appropriate or proper for you is an independent decision to be taken by you. In no event should the content of this book be construed as an express or an implied promise, guarantee or implication that you will profit or that losses can or will be limited in any manner whatsoever. Past results are no indication of future performance.

ISBN: 0615431496
ISBN-13: 9780615431499
LCCN: 2010918941

*For my mother...*

# ABOUT THE AUTHOR

Clemens Kownatzki is founder and CEO of FX Investment Strategies, a Registered Investment Advisor. In addition to running his investment advisory firm, he is a contributing author at SeekingAlpha.com and BusinessInsider.com. He also publishes the popular investment blog www.fxinvestment-strategies.com along with a weekly news-letter. In 2010, he joined Pepperdine University as an adjunct professor of finance.

Prior to starting his investment advisory business, Clemens has been in charge of the operations and risk management of two international foreign exchange and commodities brokerage firms in London and Singapore.

Clemens earned his M.B.A. degree from the Graziadio School of Business at Pepperdine University. He is also an experienced and passionate musician of many years. He graduated from Musician's Institute, Los Angeles in 1987 and was nominated Outstanding Guitar Player of the Year Award Winner.

He currently lives in California with his wife and two children.

# ACKNOWLEDGEMENTS

This book would not have been possible without the help and support of my friends and family. Here's a big thank you to all!

**To Selene:**
Thank you for teaching me to see the beauty in everything. Thanks for putting up with me throughout the lengthy writing process. You rock my world!

**To Alex and Sophia:**
You are the reason I wrote this book. Thanks for keeping me on my toes!

**To my brothers Roland and Christian:**
I would not be where I am today without you. Thanks for everything!

**To my friends and co-editors Armin Schüch, Joannie McIntyre and Sue Hoskins:**
Thank you for your thoughtful feedback and for your invaluable editorial work. You turned much of my literary guess work into coherent phrases.

**To my friends and supporters: Adam Castillo, Alex Langnau, Andreas Zachrau, Bruce Lampkov, Cecil Smith, Jonathan Merkel, Jymm Adams, Karyn Hodgens, Lenise Bent, Merlin David & M Magazine, Monica Walker, Pete Strobl, Peter Matthies & Conscious Business Institute, Pieter Vos, Phil Harrington & Youbloom.com, Randy Wiggins, Rolf Hess, Rosi Macisco, Ross Bolton, Ryan Scott Oliver, Tobias Beiner, Tom Aylesbury & Mike Packer of LA Music Academy, Ulrik Elholm and William Liu:**

Thank you for sharing your personal stories and for answering all of my persistent and annoying questions. You all brought some real-life perspectives to this project!

**To my alma mater Pepperdine University and Jim Martinoff, John Paglia, Kurt Motamedi, Maretno Agus Harjoto, Peggy Crawford, Terry Young, Wayne Strom:**

Thank you for sharing your wisdom and for contributing to my best investment ever!

# TABLE OF CONTENTS

# INTRODUCTION

## *Not Another Finance Book...*

This book project was prompted by a conversation at my family's dinner table one evening. Almost by accident, we stumbled upon the subject of finances and credit cards. During that conversation, I found out to my amazement that my teenage kids, both brilliant students with far above average numerical skills, had essentially no knowledge of how the world of finance works.

How could this be, I thought? They both excelled in school and they must have had some financial literacy training, at least in middle school, I reckoned. I was even more shocked when I learned that throughout most States in the U.S. financial literacy courses were not required in order to graduate high school. Aside from the individual efforts by some caring teachers, there is essentially nothing the school system does to prepare students for an increasingly complex financial world.

No wonder that a recent national survey by the Financial Industry Regulatory Authority (FINRA) revealed a disturbing lack of competence when it comes to basic financial literacy among US individuals. The study also indicated that younger individuals display a much lower financial literacy than older individuals.

> *"Young individuals display much lower financial literacy than older individuals. For example, a question on inflation instructed respondents to assume the annual interest on a savings account was 1% and that inflation was 2% per year. Respondents were then asked whether, after one year, they would be able to buy more than today, exactly the same, or less. Twice as many 18 to 29-year olds either answered incorrectly or stated they did not know, compared with those over age 30[1]."*

The situation for young musicians and artists is even more alarming. Since basic finance is not taught in schools, they become entrenched towards a path to the proverbial "struggling artist." The same is true for a growing number of young adults who are more likely to become self-employed, creative entrepreneurs as they try to enter the workforce or start a career.

---

1 Financial Capability in the United States. FINRA Investor Education Foundation, Dec-2009

## Challenging Times Ahead

Times could not be more critical than now. Without sounding too gloomy about future economic prospects, it is evident that the good times for many middle class Americans will have to be postponed for some years.

At the same time, most industries are in a state of constant change. More than ever, the future generations will need to think and operate like business owners if they want to be able to compete and thrive as working professionals. The days of the traditional employee with a secure job for life, generous benefits and pension plans are numbered.

All of those external conditions require a set of financial management skills in addition to being good at your craft and being an entrepreneur. Although there are hundreds of books written about Finance, Investing etc. there is much less valuable information on basic financial literacy out there. The Internet has lots of resources but most of the information is scattered across hundreds of websites.

This book is set to change all that. You will learn essential financial skills in a comprehensive and easy to read format without being intimidated.

## A Word Of Warning

This is not one of those books that promise to make you "rich in five easy steps", "within five weeks", or whatever their slogans may be. Learning and understanding finance is just like learning a new language. You can't expect to miraculously learn it in just a few days. This is a book about reality and about the hard work it takes to put your financial house in order. I do not claim to have all the answers, far from it. But as you take on this journey into the world of finance you will discover most of the fundamentals and you will learn to avoid some of the most dangerous pitfalls when it comes to handling your money.

This book does come with a small guarantee though. As a buyer of this book you will get free access to all resource material present and future. You will also be able to download any new, updated and revised editions of this book for free.

To register, just send an email to: info@moneymusic101.com

As soon as new information and updates are available, you will receive an email with download instructions.

## A Unique Approach

As both an investment advisor and a former musician, I can relate to the world of finance from an artist's perspective. It is not easy to make the transition from the abstract world of the arts to the harsh material world.

But there are many aspects of finance that are quite similar to music and the arts. Learning the basic language, understanding the rules (before you can break them) and constantly practicing your skills are but a few of the many uniting factors. It's much less about talent than it is about hard work that distinguishes the successful from the mediocre.

You don't need to be a math genius or have some special talent to become financially literate. Most of the concepts of understanding finance are rooted in an ability to appreciate basic numerical concepts. A few very fundamental math concepts need to be learned and practiced just as any artist must practice his/her craft before embarking on a career in the industry.

You will be introduced to the money skills that are critical to becoming financially literate and making a living as a self-employed individual. This book will provide a comprehensive plan to acquire those essential money skills. They will help you prevail as a manager of your financial life.

You will learn the financial strategies that will set you apart from those who live from paycheck to paycheck. The examples and analogies used in the book are both fun and thought-provoking.

## Why This Is Important To Me

My passion towards promoting financial literacy skills is only rivaled by my sincere and deep appreciation for music and the arts.

This book started out as a simple handbook that I was going to give to my kids and some of their friends. After some initial writing however, I felt this book should be geared towards musicians and artists because they were typically under-served in terms of money matters. But on closer reflection, this book is also for any young adult entering the work force or about to head for college. Anyone considering a career as a self-employed creative entrepreneur and even those who just wish to brush up on their basic financial literacy skills will find extremely good value in this book.

One last thought. My rationale was to get you, my dear reader, to understand your own personal financial situation and to enable you to live within your means. My hope has always been to elevate more people to the ranks of "working musicians" and "working artists." If I did my job right with this book, you could devote much more time towards developing your craft rather than having to wait tables or work odd jobs. Music and all arts might experience a whole new renaissance. When that happens, my mission will be accomplished.

# PREFACE

## *How It All Started...*

### Kitchen Economics

For as long as I can remember, I have been curious about how stuff worked. Musical instruments, amplifiers, speakers and stereos sparked my interest at an early age. But I also wondered about other stuff. Why, for instance, did my grandmother's food taste so much better than any other food I had? Was it the selection of ingredients or a special skill or talent?

It was either curiosity or it may have been those cold winter days that drove me into the warmth of grandma's kitchen where I spent countless hours observing, practicing and putting the various pieces of the cooking puzzle together. Some of my most vivid memories are those of sitting around the kitchen table, peeling potatoes, chopping onions and preparing food. It was then, that I also learned some of the most powerful lessons about money – you might call it lessons in kitchen economics.

As I got better at understanding the basics of food preparation, the question of budgeting invariably came up. Grandma sure knew how to budget. It was critical to know how to select the right produce, find the best value for money and conserve food if she wanted to stay within her modest budget. Like so many of her generation (her husband was killed in WWII), my grandmother had to raise three children on her own. Money was always tight but she managed to have enough savings to afford a simple but decent lifestyle.

Throughout this informal apprenticeship of cooking and kitchen economics, she would hammer two simple rules in my head.

> *Rule 1:*
> *If you want to learn how to save money, learn it from the truly rich people. The truly rich remain rich because they spend less than they have.*
>
> *Rule 2:*
> *When you have $10 in your pocket, try your best to only spend $8. Never ever spend more than $9.*

These rules stayed with me ever since and influenced all of my financial decisions. This simple concept of frugality was a guiding principle when it came to evaluating spending, taking on personal debt and dealing with banks and credit cards.

My career took a number of turns from music to finance and back to somewhere in between these two worlds. I was fortunate to live and work in Europe, Middle East/North Africa, Asia and the United States. But no matter where I lived or which industry I worked in, I noticed the amount of money people earned was relatively insignificant in terms of having enough financial resources to enjoy a decent lifestyle (nor was it in any way correlated to their happiness). Some people with relatively modest incomes were better at budgeting and saving than those who had suddenly made big money in a short period of time. I have worked with people who earned high six-figure bonuses one year only to blow those dollars on silly gadgets and fancy cars. Rather painful for some, they came up short the next year when the expected six-figure bonus didn't materialize.

In preparation for this book, I interviewed numerous artists and musicians many of which had admitted their struggles with money. There were those who are now in their 40s and 50s and practically lived from paycheck to paycheck all their lives. But I also talked to quite a few who had earned serious money over the years but never managed to save more than a few months' worth of living expenses, not to mention, any investments, pension plans or property.

Yet, I have met a number of working musicians who have been able to make a decent living through hard work, dedication and by managing their personal finances effectively. As you go through this book, you will see examples of good and bad money habits. More than anything, it's the good habits that make you a financially successful individual. I can show you the tools needed to get financially ahead. You must make the choice to adopt these tools and transform them into good money habits to make this a win/win situation for you and for me.

**How To Get The Most Out Of This Book**
This book is using a bottom-up approach in the way the material is presented. Chapter One gives you a bit of a historic background about money and banking. Chapter Two is a review of basic math concepts like interest and the time value of money. If you already learned about the history of money, how banks evolved and how to do basic money math, feel free to jump forward to Chapter Three. That's when we dive right into practical applications such as handling your bank accounts, dealing with credit cards, loans, budgeting and developing your own financial plan. Finally, we discuss investments and learn how to develop a simple but effective financial plan.

When going through this book, I would encourage you to take lots of mental breaks and carefully read the sections called *"Think about it."* Those are brief notes not only helping you to digest what you just read but also giving you a different perspective on things.

Don't forget to register by sending an email to info@moneymusic101.com. Registration will give you access to additional tools, information as well as free access to new editions of the book once available.

Lastly, check out the resource section at the end of the book. You will find links to useful websites, online tools and book recommendations.

Enough said, let's get started with Money Music 101.

# ONE

## The History Of Money & Banking

### What Is Money?

Dollars, Euros, Pesos, Pounds, Yen, Swiss Francs and many other currencies are some of today's denominations of what we commonly refer to as "Money". In the U.S., the only accepted currency as a form of payment is called the U.S. Dollar.

One dollar might mean something to you in terms of what you can buy with it, sadly not all that much these days, but what exactly is money?

Money is often referred to as a **medium of exchange** which means that you can exchange your money for things like food, a little more of your money for an iPod, cell phone or a guitar and lots more for bigger things like cars, trucks or houses.

People use money to buy all sorts of things but they also need money to pay for all their living expenses including housing, taxes, insurances, utilities – the list goes on. Most of us exchange our money not just to buy things but we also "exchange" our Dollars, Euros or Pesos for entertainment, going to the movies, Disney Land, eating out at fancy restaurants or generally going shopping at our favorite stores.

Money does not just buy things and services though. It is also considered a sort of measurement, a yardstick or as some people say, a "barometer of success." People with lots of money are called rich and there are many examples of rich and famous people; just open the glossy magazines or read the lists in financial magazines like Fortune 500 or Forbes to learn how much money some people were able to amass.

> ### Think About It:
> You might wonder where the word money came from. Legend has it that the temple of Juno "Moneta" was the place where coins and money were stored in ancient Rome. Moneta is the Latin and Italian word for money, coins and cash.

One can never have enough money, so it seems, and the advertising media have become very efficient at making us all feel bad for not having all that much money. They make us crave for the latest gadgets like new iPhones, new computers or the latest fashion accessory of the time.

With all that media pressure and advertising bombarding us 24/7, temptation is high to spend every bit of our hard earned Dollars and more.

That is exactly where another kind of money appears, in the form of credit. Credit is indeed a form of money and it has been replacing paper money and coins by leaps and bounds.

Here are a few fun money facts to get your heart racing:
If you could count all the coins and dollar bills that we all have in our pockets, under the mattresses or in safety deposit boxes, including all the bills and coins sitting in banks you would come up with a lot of money – close to one trillion dollars.

Yes, there are some people in the U.S. government who keep track of how much physical money or currency is floating around at any given moment. That amount of money floating around is called currency in circulation. One trillion dollars is $1,000,000,000,000 (12 zeros) which is obviously a huge pile of money. No worries, we will learn a lot more about large numbers and how to deal with them later on.

But for now, digest an even bigger number, how about:

$15,000,000,000,000 ($15 trillion)

That is roughly the value of all money in goods and services produced within the U.S. in a year, 15 times bigger than the total value of all coins and bank notes currently in circulation. This also means that there is 15 times more value produced each year than we can carry in our pockets and keep in our mattresses, safe deposit boxes and all the banks and their bills and coins.

You might call all this other money electronic money. The same electronic money appears in form of digits and numbers on your bank statement, your pay slip, your ATM print out or your brokerage statement but it is also included in all the credit and debit card transactions that we all have been using more and more in the past few decades.

### Practicality rules
Money is not just an efficient medium of exchange it can also be a store of value. It is easier to keep $100 in your pocket rather than storing $100 worth of your favorite fruit at home let alone having to move around with those heavy bags of fruit. The fruit might spoil whereas your money won't.

As an accounting or measuring unit with clearly defined qualities, money is ideal to keep track of and compare values with other goods making financial planning and investing even possible.

And, rightly or wrongly, money can give a sense of security. People who don't have much money and live from pay-check to pay-check, and those who wish they even had one, believe that more money would make their lives more secure. Almost everyone has the natural tendency to want more money primarily for this (false) sense of security. As we will find out later in this book, it is not what you earn but what you keep that makes all the difference.

∾

# A Brief History Of Money

Having learned what money is we can now take a look at the history of money. When and where did it all begin?

The sources differ slightly as to the exact years and origin of what we consider today's money. But it is fair to say that the history of money is a few thousand years old.

### Barter

Before the advent of money in a form somewhat similar to today's coins and bank notes, barter was the earliest form of payment. Barter is also called a trade or exchange of one good for another. In ancient times, various types of goods and animals were exchanged. In the early civilizations of today's Middle East about 2000 years B.C., goats, camels, sheep and grains were exchanged for other goods. Trade was conducted primarily on a negotiated basis; that meant you had to haggle for some time before you could get what you wanted. A camel might have been worth 20 sheep, or 15 goats. One goat might also buy you a month's worth of grains to feed the family.

In ancient Egypt, things were a bit more organized and prices were known throughout the country according to official price lists. Standard sacks of grain were used to pay workers; a typical worker might have earned 5½ sacks (200kg or 400lb) of grain per month while a foreman might earn 7½ sacks (250kg or 550lb)[2].

Throughout the centuries many different forms of goods were traded but eventually, people figured out that schlepping around heavy sacks of grain or transporting camels, cows and goats was not the most efficient way of trading. For instance, finding someone who had exactly what you wanted and, at the same time was willing to exchange that for goods you had to offer, was time consuming and unproductive. If no deal took place, your goods may have spoiled or livestock may have died during transport leaving you with a potential loss.

---

2 Source: http://en.wikipedia.org/wiki/Ancient_Egypt

Another problem with barter was the difficulty to agree on a price. What if the grains you needed were worth a goat and a half? What if the plow you wanted would cost you say 1.5 horses?

> ### *Think About It:*
> *Imagine if you had to go back to the barter system. What if you needed a new mobile phone but all you had was a collection of was a collection of guitars? Ready to unscrew a guitar neck in exchange for a mobile phone? As a drummer, would you exchange 20 drum sticks for a new snare drum skin? How would you barter strings for a violin? And if you are a painter, would you give away one of your paintings in exchange for some paints and a canvas?*

You get the point. In those early days, making a living was not an easy affair. Any business transaction was a complicated and time consuming ordeal of moving around heavy, perishable, and often difficult to manage goods including live-stock. Worse yet, there was no guarantee that you could ever get your hands on the goods you needed or that an agreeable price was even achievable (remember the 1.5 horse dilemma?).

### Early Money

The solution came along in the form of Bartering 2.0 when the first ancient forms of money were created. Salt, elephant hair and ivory were the earliest signs of money used in Africa[3].

In ancient China, knives, chisels and certain types of shells were used as forms of payment.

Other cultures used rocks, cowry shells, beads, gem stones, tobacco, spices, and eventually scarce and precious metals were introduced as standard forms of payments. The various types of commodities were used as a replacement for money which is why this early money is often called commodity money.

---

3 Kenneth Morris & Alan Siegel, Guide to Understanding Money & Investing, Lightbulb Press, 1993, p. 5

**Think About It:**
*In times of crises (war, natural disasters, hyper-inflation) bartering often resurfaces. When all else fails, you cannot eat money. In those situations, various types of food (preferably non-perishables), medical supplies as well as cigarettes and alcohol have been found to be superior to paper money or credit cards.*

### Metal Coins as Standard of Payment

As more and more countries and regions began interacting with each other either through war, invasions or the expansion of trade routes, metal coins became the preferred form of payment. Coins made from precious metals such as gold, silver, copper and bronze were considered most valuable because they could easily be melted again and converted into its pure metal form. These early metal coins had an inherent value, which is the value by weight of their precious metal content.

But metal coins also had another significant advantage which made the use of it spread so fast throughout the ancient world. Unlike the typical goods used in the old barter system, they did not rot or die during transport. Coins essentially last forever.

After Christopher Columbus had discovered the New World the Spanish Conquistadores captured vast amounts of gold and silver bullion which led to an increased use of gold and silver coins in Europe. Spain's coinage system introduced in 1497 provided the first national coinage for Spain.[4] Around the same time, a Silver mine in Joachimsthal (Bohemia) was one of the largest producers of silver. One of their silver coins, the Joachimsthaler[5] turned into the generic name "Thaler" which is where the name "Dollar" originated from.

With the spread of the Thaler and other silver and gold coins throughout Europe, official coinage by a country or state helped further improve commerce and trade. By that time, standardized coinage was the norm. The coins were available in various denominations such as 1,2,5,and 10 Thalers all of which differed in size, weight and sometimes precious metal content.

### The Arrival of Paper Money

Even before the English goldsmiths and the Italian bankers came up with credit notes and bills of exchange, paper money was introduced in China

---

4 Money: A History. Edited by Jonathan Williams, St. Martin's Press, New York, 1997, p. 165
5 Money: A History. Edited by Jonathan Williams, St. Martin's Press, New York, 1997, p. 163

during the Yuan Dynasty (1206-1367)[6]. But it took a few more centuries until the first freely circulating bank notes came about. It was not the Bank of England (founded in 1694) but the Riksbank of Sweden founded in 1668 which is considered to be the oldest central bank in the world[7]. Since then, central banks in many countries around the world are responsible for issuing paper money as well as being entrusted with regulating banks and controlling the supply of money both in paper, coins as well as in credit form.

**Think About It:**
*The first paper money appeared in China during the Yuan dynasty and today's Chinese currency is still called the "Chinese Yuan".*

Today, electronic forms of payment including credit cards form the vast majority of all financial transactions. Electronic payment methods have been one of the cornerstones of the growth of global business transactions. Bank notes and coins are still the most common form of physical money today. But gold and silver are also considered rare and valuable commodities retaining some of the important qualities of money.

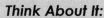

**Think About It:**
*Gold has been a form of money for centuries. The value of this precious metal has fluctuated over time but has steadily kept up with inflation. In the early part of the 21st century, the value of gold has increased to over $1,400 per ounce. Can you see a potential issue of using gold as money? How would you pay for small ticket items like a sandwich or a cup of coffee?*

In summary, the origins of money go back thousands of years. Barter was the first form of payment, simply by exchanging one good for another. Replacement of goods in the form of commodity money made trade and barter easier. Salt, elephant hair, ivory, knives, chisels, rocks, cowry shells, beads, gem stones, tobacco and spices were all forms of commodity money. Scarce and precious metals were introduced as standard forms of payments. Coins eventually replaced commodity money and the first coinages gained massive popularity during the Middle Ages because of vast new sources of gold and silver.

---

6 Money: A History. Edited by Jonathan Williams, St. Martin's Press, New York, 1997, p. 177
7 http://www.riksbank.com

**Money Trivia:**
*Earlier, we learned that the name dollar originated from "Thaler". Although the use of dollars predates the Declaration of Independence, a realistic starting point for official issuance of dollars came with the Coinage Act of 1792 which enacted that "the money of account of the United States shall be expressed in dollars".[8]*

༖

# A Brief History Of Banking

The history of banking very much ties into the history of money. Both have been going hand in hand ever since barter has been replaced by the first forms of commodity money as a method of payment.

As with the origins of money, there are no exact dates as to when banking started but the best references about early forms of banking appear around 1750 B.C. in the Code of Hammurabi, which also set out rules for lending.

Centuries later in ancient Egypt, a centralized banking system accepted grain deposits as a form of money. With branches all over the country, this predecessor of modern banking allowed the transfer of funds from an account in one city to another an account in another city without any money (grain) changing hands. Imagine how ingenious that system must have been operating more than 2000 years before the invention of computers and online banking.

It took yet another 1000 years before a new milestone in the history of banking appeared. The Crusades, starting around 1100 A.D., highlighted the need for more banking and payment transfer services. In order to support entire armies sent from Central Europe to the Middle East quick transfers of payments were needed to buy supplies, equipment and keep the soldiers well-fed and well-paid. Larger amounts were needed to make sure certain alliances and treaties with other rulers (e.g. free passage through a region or country) were actually upheld.

---

8 Source: www.usmint.gov/historianscorner

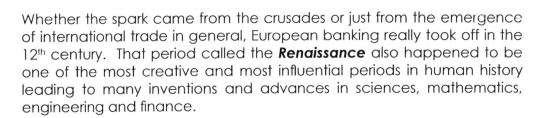

> ## Think About It:
> It's interesting how the history of money and banking directly ties into the history of politics, governments and wars. The Knights Templar, famously depicted in the novel DaVinci Code by Dan Brown, was a military order that arose out of the First Crusade. A believer of conspiracy theories might come up with a good explanation as to how the Knights Templar may have directly been involved in the first international banks. Assuming this order still exists now, albeit in secrecy, they might still be involved in the highest circles of finance even today...

Whether the spark came from the crusades or just from the emergence of international trade in general, European banking really took off in the 12th century. That period called the **Renaissance** also happened to be one of the most creative and most influential periods in human history leading to many inventions and advances in sciences, mathematics, engineering and finance.

The Medici of Venice started international merchant banking services very similar to the services offered by banks today. Banking houses like the Medici or the Fuggers of Augsburg were the most well-known and among the most powerful merchant banking dynasties ever. Compared to today, the Medici family was probably more powerful than the largest financial institutions we know now. For their time, they were also extremely innovative like organizations such as Google, Microsoft and Apple today.

In addition to finding new methods of accounting for interest and devising rules for loan repayments, the banking houses also created so called "Bills of Exchange" which allowed their clients to transact business at a bank in another country.

First full banking services to the general public were offered by the Bank of Barcelona, Spain. This bank accepted deposits, made loans, and arranged payments in currencies of other countries.

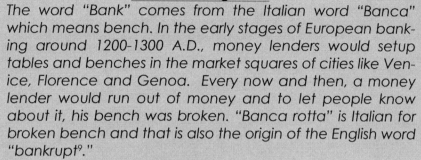

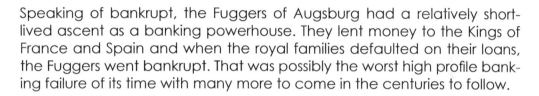

**Some Banking Trivia**
*The word "Bank" comes from the Italian word "Banca" which means bench. In the early stages of European banking around 1200-1300 A.D., money lenders would setup tables and benches in the market squares of cities like Venice, Florence and Genoa. Every now and then, a money lender would run out of money and to let people know about it, his bench was broken. "Banca rotta" is Italian for broken bench and that is also the origin of the English word "bankrupt[9]."*

Speaking of bankrupt, the Fuggers of Augsburg had a relatively short-lived ascent as a banking powerhouse. They lent money to the Kings of France and Spain and when the royal families defaulted on their loans, the Fuggers went bankrupt. That was possibly the worst high profile banking failure of its time with many more to come in the centuries to follow.

The Medici by contrast diversified and had family members involved in all areas of business, art, politics and the church (three members of the Medici clan became Pope) helping them to retain their power for several centuries.

Let's shift gears now and move over to England where in the early 1600s, the London goldsmiths expanded the concepts of deposits, withdrawals and money lending. Although some early forms of paper money was available as early as the 13th century in China, the goldsmiths came up with a brilliant idea that marked the beginning of paper money as we know it today.

Gold has always been a symbol of money and wealth. Throughout the ages, wealthy people, nobles and businessmen kept large amounts of their fortune in gold bars. As you can imagine, the gold bars aren't exactly ideal to do the basic business transactions. It wasn't that easy to cut them in half (to pay for smaller amounts) and they were too heavy to carry around all the time. In response to that, the goldsmiths offered a new service wherein they accepted gold from their clients for safe keeping and issued paper receipts for the deposits. Soon, the owners of those receipts noticed that it was much more convenient to use these paper receipts to directly pay for their goods and the sellers of goods found comfort in the fact that the paper receipts were placeholders of the actual gold deposits with the goldsmiths. Paper money was born and here is an example of how it worked:

Meet Henry a young merchant in medieval London. Henry had $1,000 worth of gold which he deposited with Mr. Goldsmith, the banker. Mr. Goldsmith gave Henry a paper receipt for the $1,000 gold deposit.

9 DK Eyewitness Books-Economy, Johnny Acton and David Goldblatt, 2010, Page 24

Henry later on used the receipt to purchase $1,000 worth of grains and supplies from Billy the farmer. The exchange of the paper receipt replaced the direct exchange of gold and made the business transaction easier and faster. Billy the farmer was now the legal owner of the $1,000 worth of gold which was still on deposit with Mr. Goldsmith. And Henry was happy he didn't have to drag around his gold bars to pay for his grains. It turned to be a win-win situation for everyone.

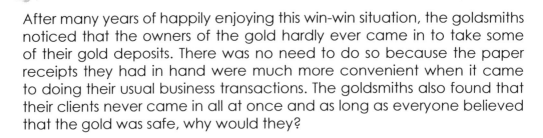

### Think About It:
*In the above example, both Henry and Billy found this method of doing business very convenient. They didn't mind paying a fee to the banker for offering this service. All in all, it was a true win-win situation for everyone. But despite being paid a nice fee for accepting gold deposits from clients, goldsmiths felt there might be a way to generate even more fees. We will find out shortly how another, perhaps more brilliant idea, generated a lot more money for the goldsmiths. Before reading further, take a good guess what kind of idea they might have had.*

After many years of happily enjoying this win-win situation, the goldsmiths noticed that the owners of the gold hardly ever came in to take some of their gold deposits. There was no need to do so because the paper receipts they had in hand were much more convenient when it came to doing their usual business transactions. The goldsmiths also found that their clients never came in all at once and as long as everyone believed that the gold was safe, why would they?

This observation lead to the most significant invention of banking and money lending ever conceived. The goldsmiths found that they could issue new paper receipts to people who needed money without them actually having any gold deposits. In essence, they could make loans, charge interest on those loans and create new paper money out of nothing more than the belief that whatever amount was stated on these paper receipts was good and could be exchanged for the same amount in gold at any given time. The goldsmiths created the money they loaned and generated a new source of income much more powerful and profitable than the small fees they received from the gold safety deposits. The goldsmiths and all bankers from that moment in time learned very quickly that they could create new money from new paper receipts and enjoyed a source of income that was rooted in the power of compound interest. In essence that is how banks still operate today, of course within the rules and guidelines of the law.

The 1600s also gave birth to another important milestone in banking. The first central bank was the Riksbank of Sweden founded in 1668[10]. Soon after,

---

10 http://www.riksbank.com

the Bank of England was established in 1694[11] and the Bank of France was the first French central bank founded in 1800. It took yet another century until the US Federal Reserve Bank with its system of 12 regional branches was established in 1914.

### More Banking Trivia:

*Although the Bank of England was founded in 1694, it has only had a monopoly to issue banknotes since the early 20th century. More surprisingly, it is only since 1997 that the central bank has had a legal responsibility for setting the UK's official interest rate.*

Today, every country has its own central bank. Central banks are responsible for regulating all other banks. You could say they are the banking police, but they also control the supply of money both in paper, coin as well as in credit form. By making sure that there is always enough (but not too much) money and credit available and by setting interest rates, central banks help to navigate each country's economy.

### Think About It:

*Ever since the first banks have been established, banking and money lending was a profitable business. But it also happened that banks went bust as we learned from the first high profile bank failure during the Renaissance period. When bank managers were not careful or when they loaned too much money to questionable borrowers, banks could go bust. The stock market crash and subsequent Great Depression in 1929 saw more bank failures than ever before in history. It wasn't just that people lost fortunes in the stock market, regular folks saw their savings disappear when banks closed and could not repay their customers. This prompted the need for some safety measures so that savers were insured that their money was safe with a bank. Along with many other new rules for banking, finance and stock markets, the FDIC (Federal Deposit Insurance Corporation) was created in 1933 to insure bank accounts with a guaranteed amount that would be repaid in case a bank went bust. The initial insurance coverage was $2500 in 1934 but that amount was subsequently raised numerous times. Today, the FDIC coverage amount is $250,000 for each account. Why do you think that amount has been raised by a factor of 100 since then?*

---

11 http://www.bankofengland.co.uk

# How Banks Operate Today

In the second half of the 20th century, banks expanded further from small regional banks to worldwide international institutions with branches in numerous countries. Payment systems enabling the instantaneous transfers of funds anywhere in the world played a big role leading to the globalization of business in the second half of the 20th century.

Advances in technology and new innovations lead to the birth of credit cards, Automated Teller Machines (ATM) and eventually online banking as we know it. Today, bank customers seldom set foot inside a bank unless they need to personally talk to a banker for complicated transactions like business loans or mortgages. Everything else can be done faster and more conveniently at ATMs or via online banking anytime day or night.

Today, a few banks started up as pure online banks without any branches. Although most people are somewhat suspicious whether these banks are real - i.e. not having the traditional bank buildings with tellers and safes - these banks can sometimes offer better terms because of the cost savings from operating purely online.

Few people realize however, that modern banks do very little business in the bank branches today. In dollar amounts, the majority of their income is no longer from traditional banking but from investment banking, trading and other financial services. You may have seen a glimpse of these trading and investment activities when some of the biggest banks had problems during the financial crisis of 2008/2009 also referred to as the Great Recession. It became clear that some banks took on too much risk and engaged in risky trades that should have not been touched by traditional banks.

But despite the recent financial crisis, the banking and financial services industries are destined to evolve and continue to innovate creating new financial products.

### *Think About It:*
*What other innovations in banking can you foresee? With the advances in computer technology, can you imagine a time when cash will completely disappear? What percentage of all your financial transactions is done with cash today? Think of some of the consequences if cash no longer exists.*

# Timeline

**1750 B.C.**
The Code of Hammurabi documents rules for banking and money lending.

**320 B.C.**
Grain banks in Ancient Egypt had a system to transfer funds from one city to another.

**1095-1270 A.D.**
The Crusades required a system of quick transfer of payments to foreign countries.

**1401 A.D.**
The Bank of Barcelona provided the first basic banking services.

**1600s**
The London goldsmiths issued paper receipts for deposits in gold.

**1668 A.D.**
The Riksbank of Sweden was the first central bank.

**1694**
The Bank of England was founded.

**1914**
The US Federal Reserve Bank was created.

**October 24, 1929**
Black Thursday - stock market crash and start of the great depression

**1933**
Creation of the Securities Exchange Commission (SEC) and FDIC

**1950**
Diners Club created the first charge card

**1958**
American Express launched their first national credit card.

**1972**
The Automatic Teller Machine was invented

**1990s**
With the emergence of the Internet, online banking services started.

**2008/2009**
Biggest financial crisis since the Great Depression.

# TWO

## Basic Numbers Concepts & Money Math

### Most Dreaded Subject: The Numbers...

I realize it may be boring, painful, and perhaps frightening for some of you reading this. Yes, we could talk about savings, budgets, financial plans and investing all day long. But unless the basic numbers make sense to you, your financial life might turn out to be a trial and error kind of roller coaster that could be painful, even devastating. You need to understand basic numbers to get a grip on your finances.

> ### Think About It:
> *As a saxophone player and Jazz enthusiast, would you ever consider learning a Charlie Parker solo without first learning some basic scales? A composer could not possibly consider writing an orchestral symphony without understanding the basics of harmony. If you were an architect, would you be able to function without having at least a basic understanding of statics and the strength of materials?*

No matter how you look at it, you have to be able to understand the basics of simple math to truly grasp some of the fundamentals of personal financial management – the Money 101 stuff. If you want to become a financially responsible and self-sustaining individual, here's the first step you need to take. Because it's painful, we're doing this at the beginning of this book.

But fear not; all of the math can easily be done with basic arithmetic, most of which you probably learned as early as 5th grade. It's all very simple stuff like addition, multiplication, division and percentages.

You may be surprised how much you already know about numbers and how we can practice ways to put numbers into different contexts. The objective of this unit is to first get you re-acquainted with numbers and then use your numerical skills in the world of Money 101.

Let's get started!

# Review Of Fractions & Percentages

This may sound trivial but the most basic and never-ending form of math and numbers sense is counting.

We deal with numbers all the time and in many different ways we just don't realize that we actually possess some important numerical skills that are such an important aspect of financial literacy.

We won't actually go back to Addition, Subtraction, Multiplication and Division; there are many helpful websites where you can practice some of these basic computational skills. Just do a search for elementary or basic math. Dealing with fractions however is a bit less intuitive for some of us. Let's look at the very basic forms of fractions for a moment.

The easiest way to look at fractions is with the help of the good old pie chart. A pie is split into 2, 4, 8 equal parts giving you a visual overview of how fractions work.

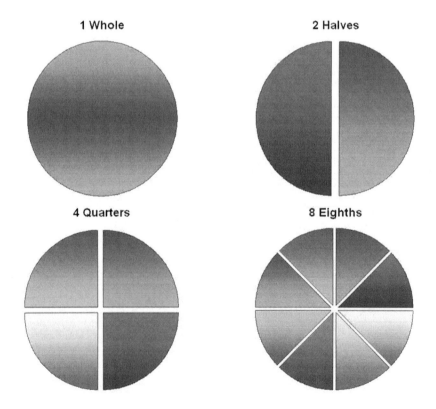

All we did in elementary school was to write these graphical images into numbers such as $\frac{1}{2}$, $\frac{1}{4}$, $\frac{1}{8}$ etc. There's not much more to it.

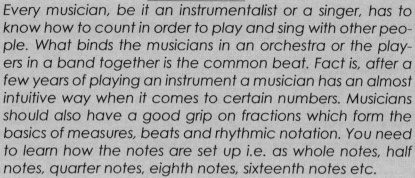

**Think About It:**
*Every musician, be it an instrumentalist or a singer, has to know how to count in order to play and sing with other people. What binds the musicians in an orchestra or the players in a band together is the common beat. Fact is, after a few years of playing an instrument a musician has an almost intuitive way when it comes to certain numbers. Musicians should also have a good grip on fractions which form the basics of measures, beats and rhythmic notation. You need to learn how the notes are set up i.e. as whole notes, half notes, quarter notes, eighth notes, sixteenth notes etc.*

### From Fractions To Percentages

Associating fractions with visual aids like pie charts helps us to get a feel for these numbers. The next step would be to use our knowledge of fractions and convert them into decimals and percentages. It is important to remember that "percent" means "per hundred" but it also means that it is part of a whole.

When dealing with more complex financial percentage calculations, I usually go back to my basic pie charts. They give me an immediate sense of how much of a total each percentage point looks like in the bigger picture. For instance, divide a pie into 4 equal pieces to get 4 quarters.

Here in the U.S., we are fortunate to have coins based on the same quarter system, the 25 cent piece also known as "the quarter". You might remember your first encounter with money from getting some coins. You learned early on in life, either from your teachers or from the tooth fairy, that 4 quarters make up 1 Dollar. Write it out as a decimal:

***

**1 quarter equals $0.25 or 25% of 1 Dollar**

***

You might also vaguely recall that you need 10 dimes (10 x 10 cents) to have a Dollar.

***

**10 cents spelled out is: $0.10 or 10% of one Dollar**

***

# Fractions, Percentages & Ratios

Having converted fractions into decimals and percentages, there is one other code word which is often used as a measurement in personal finance. It is called the "ratio". Ratios are often used to analyze financial statements and investment performances.

Ratios are somewhat similar to fractions but let's look at some examples so we can differentiate them better:

Let's say you have 2 girls and 3 guys playing in your band; the number of girls versus guys can be expressed as the **ratio 2:3**. The ratio therefore compares two quantities directly.

The total number of players in your band is 5.  Using that total helps us to explain your band make-up in terms of fractions. 2/5 of your band members are female whereas 3/5 are male.  Let's convert these fractions into decimals and percentages.

| | |
|---|---|
| Girls: | 2/5 = 0.4 or  40% |
| Guys: | 3/5 = 0.6 or  60% |
| **Totals:** | **5/5 = 1.0 or 100%** |

Let's look at another example to see some of the limitations of ratios.

In the same band, you have 2 guitar players, 1 bass player, 1 drummer and 1 keyboard player. Ratios don't really work well in terms of expressing the make-up of instrument players in your band.

But you can easily see how fractions and percentages are better to express the make up or the proportions in your band. Here's how percentages work when you analyze the distribution of the individual players in a band as compared with the entire band:

| | |
|---|---|
| Guitars: | 2/5 or 40% |
| Bass: | 1/5 or 20% |
| Drums: | 1/5 or 20% |
| Keyboard: | 1/5 or 20% |
| **Totals:** | **5/5 or 100%** |

You can see now that fractions and percentages are ideal to show how each part relates to the entire group as a whole - in this case your band. Ratios are more useful when comparing just two numbers or quantities directly.

## Ratios For Musicians & Sound Engineers

One area of music where these concepts come in handy is harmonics.

Harmonics play a very important role with string instruments. As we know, the strings in those instruments vibrate at a certain frequency. When properly tuned, the open A string of a violin vibrates at 440 Hz (up/down swings per second). The open string is also called the fundamental or first harmonic. Taking a snapshot of these swings, the sound wave of the vibrating string looks something like this:

To get the 2nd harmonic of that string, you probably know the drill: At half the length of your string is the 2nd harmonic. For guitars and basses, that is exactly at the 12th fret. By halving your string and placing your finger at the spot (just gently without pressing it down on the fret board) you get two equal waves which are half the length but vibrate (oscillate) at twice the frequency of the open string. In the case of an open A string on a violin, this would also be an A vibrating at 880 Hz (2 x 440 = 880) exactly one octave above the open string A and it looks something like this:

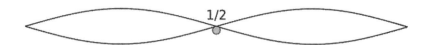

Your next harmonic, at one third of the length of the open string returns three equal waves, one third of the length each but vibrating at three times the frequency. This harmonic is one octave + a perfect 5th above the open string A.

You can continue on with this to get more harmonics and with a bit of practice, you can go all the way to the third octave above the open string. But let's get back to fractions, percentages and ratios. In terms of the fractions, you can obviously see how parting the wavelength of a string renders different kinds of fractions. By now you should be able to convert all these fractions to percentages too.

To illustrate ratios, let us look at how one harmonic relates to another and what interval corresponds to which ratio.

The interval between the open string, the first harmonic, and the second harmonic is an octave. We can generate that octave at 1/2 of the length of the open string. It just so happens that the ratio between open string and first harmonic is also 1:2. Expressed as frequencies, the open A string vibrates at 440 Hz and the second harmonic vibrates 880 Hz. The ratio again is 1:2 or double the original frequency. You can now continue to examine the ratios between the harmonics and note down the resulting tone intervals as follows:

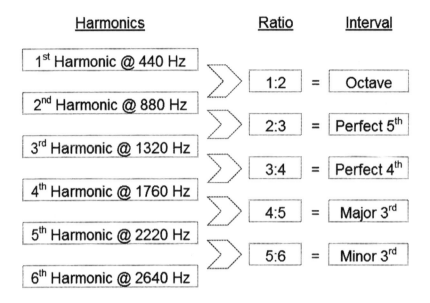

But let's go back to reality now since this is a financial literacy book not a music theory book. Hopefully, you get the picture from doing these exercises. There are countless ways in which you can bring some basic math into your daily life and develop a feel for numbers.

A "feel for numbers" you might ask? Yes, just like a painter has to develop an intuitive sense for shapes and colors, just like a musician must develop a feel for rhythm and a sense of time, a financially savvy individual must also develop a feel for basic numbers.

Although some accountants and financial gurus might disagree with me here, I firmly believe that there is such a thing as a financial gut feeling based on the understanding and practice of dealing with numbers and money in general. Practice is a routine that makes you better. Nobody is born to be a finance whiz or a great money manager. You have to learn it and keep practicing so it becomes second nature to you.

Knowing how to deal with numbers and how to handle money by using some basic numerical skills can save you a bundle of money. More importantly, it provides a good foundation for your financial future. It just might allow you to become a better artist and excel in your job too.

No matter how you look at it, you have to be able to understand the basics of simple math to truly grasp some of the fundamentals of personal financial management – the Money 101 stuff.  If you want to become a financially responsible and more successful, here's the first step you need to take:

**Know your numbers and learn how to use them to your advantage.**

∾

# Interest: History and Concept

### What Is Interest?
Do a search on the internet and you may come up with a number of definitions, somewhere along these lines:

> *Interest is the price borrowers pay for using someone else's money – Federalreserve.gov*
>
> *A charge for the privilege of borrowing money, typically expressed as an annual percentage rate – Investopedia.com*

I like to think of interest as a way of making money from money or, as some say, letting your money grow. The downside of interest is also true for the person who has to pay interest. Paying interest is a way of losing money from owing money.

Today, everybody borrows and lends money all the time. Since there is no free money out there, we all have to deal with interest in one form or another.  Here are some examples:

- You can receive interest from your savings account
- A student has to pay back his student loan with interest
- Credit card companies charge high interest on balances
- A musician might buy a new instrument on credit
- Families taking on a home loan pay interest to the lender
- A couple gets dividends from investing in a Treasury Bond

### How It All Started
The earliest references for interest date back several thousand years as a Google timeline search reveals. The first set of laws dealing with borrowing something against interest was in the Code of Hammurabi ca. 1750 BC. Hammurabi, the King of Babylon, set out various rules for borrowing and repayment in form of grains. The concept however, was quite different from today's money lending. Borrowing was typically meant for production

of goods only. For example, a landowner would rent his land to be cultivated and the tenant or borrower would pay back the landowner in grains.

A notable distinction was that the landowner and tenant were sort of partners with the landowner having an "interest" in the field producing enough crops to make a return for both lender and borrower. Unlike today's lending for the payment of interest, if the tenant was not able to produce any crops, the landowner simply did not get paid.

> *48. If a man owe a debt, and Adad (i.e. the Storm God) inundate his field and carry away the produce, or, through lack of water, grain have not grown in the field, in that year he shall not make any return of grain to the creditor, he shall alter his contract tablet, and he shall not pay the interest for that year.*[12]

As you can see, the concept of borrowing and debt is not a new one. When landowners figured out how easy it was to make money from lending, greed and abusive interest charges surfaced as well. The notion of usury, which regarded interest as unfair and sinful, started to appear in historic text books. Most religions have devised rules against usury as found in religious text books. Even today, the Koran explicitly forbids interest.

The Greek philosopher Aristotle (384-322 BC) was very influential in forming a view against usury that is still relevant today. In his view, money was lifeless and, unlike a cow that could beget more cows, was not in itself able to produce more money. In his explanation of "wealth-getting," he had the following to say about usury:

> *The most hated sort and with the greatest reason, is usury, which makes a gain out of money itself, and not from the natural object of it. For money was intended to be used in exchange but not to increase at interest. And this term interest, which means the birth of money from money, is applied to the breeding of money because the offspring resembles the parent. Wherefore of all modes of getting wealth, this is the most unnatural.*[13]

### Interest Throughout History

The earliest forms of interest involved simple interest calculations. But even then, it was not uncommon that a lender might take advantage of a poor peasant by charging unreasonably high interest on a loan. That was

---

12 Code of Hammurabi, By Hammurabi (King of Babylonia.), Percy Stuart Peache Handcock, New York, The MacMillan Company 1920, Page 15
13 Politics, By Aristotle, Translated by Benjamin Jowett, Nuvision Publications, 2004, Page 19

considered usury during the early Mesopotamian civilizations of Sumer (3000 BC) and Babylon (1900 BC). The Code of Hammurabi set out clear legal limits for interest at 33 1/3% on grain and 20% on loans of silver[14].

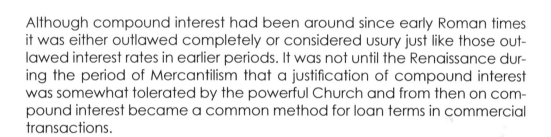

### Think About It:

*The earliest civilizations figured out that it would be unfair to people of lesser means if they were forced to pay unreasonably high interest rates to their lender. Today, most credit card companies in the US are not bound by legal interest rate limits. National credit-card issuers such as JPMorgan Chase or Bank of America base their credit-card subsidiaries in business-friendly states such as Delaware and South Dakota that do not limit interest rates[15]. Have you checked your credit card terms to see if you are paying usury rates right now?*

Although compound interest had been around since early Roman times it was either outlawed completely or considered usury just like those outlawed interest rates in earlier periods. It was not until the Renaissance during the period of Mercantilism that a justification of compound interest was somewhat tolerated by the powerful Church and from then on compound interest became a common method for loan terms in commercial transactions.

Around the same time appeared the first concise methods on calculating and recording compound interest. The Medici of Venice and the Fuggers of Augsburg were among those who recognized the power of compound interest. They were among the most powerful merchant banks of their time. "Arithmeticall Questions", written by Richard Witt in 1613, is considered to be the first book entirely dedicated to the subject of compound interest. The book included tables based on 10%, the maximum allowable rate of interest during that time.

---

14 A History of Interest Rates, Sidney Homer, Rutgers University Press, 1963, Page 31
15 Source: http://www.reuters.com/article/idUSN1910217420100519

**Think About It:**
*You may know that borrowers with better credit history can get lower interest rates. The rationale is simple: If someone is not quite as credit worthy, lenders have a higher risk that the borrower might default on a loan. The less credit worthy a borrower, the higher the rates a lender would charge. During the renaissance period in Europe, loans to Kings, Queens and other nobles were considered high risk for merchants and bankers extending those loans. In Italy in 1494, a short term loan to a Prince carried interest rates between 42-100%[16]. Kings and Princes soon realized that financing their lavish lifestyles was getting expensive at these high interest rates. Legal limits on interest were imposed. Queen Elizabeth I was the first to enforce a legal maximum of 10% in England in the late 16th century[17].*

Simple interest and compound interest calculations will be discussed in the next chapter in great detail. But before you delve into the meat of this book, I would like to give some additional food for thought.

**Think About It:**
*Albert Einstein was one of the most influential scientists of his time. His theories on relativity led to the most often quoted equation of our time: $E = mc^2$.*

*But Einstein himself thought of another discovery as far more influential. Einstein is quoted as saying:*

**"Compound Interest is the greatest mathematical discovery of all time"**

With that in mind, let us proceed and learn how to calculate interest.

∽

## Simple Interest & Compound Interest

This chapter is possibly the most important one in terms of applying essential math concepts to personal finance. We will be doing some fun exercises to help you get better at dealing with interest. Like anything else you learn, practice is essential!

16 A History of Interest Rates, Sidney Homer, Rutgers University Press, 1963, Page 110
17 A History of Interest Rates, Sidney Homer, Rutgers University Press, 1963, Page 113

I might also have a few tips and tricks up my sleeve that you can use to immediately make sense of some of the mumbo jumbo that you hear of and read about in financial news and media.

Once you understand the concepts of simple and compound interest, everything else in personal finance just falls into place.

❧

## Simple Interest

Simple interest is just like the name implies – it is simple and it involves a basic percentage calculation. Here are the components to calculate simple interest:

**I** = Interest Amount; the amount received or paid in interest.
**P** = Principal; the amount of money borrowed or invested.
**r** = Interest rate; the percentage per year a.k.a. per annum (p.a.).
**t** = Time; the length of time in years or fraction of a year.

---

Formula for calculating simple interest: **I = P** x **r** x **t**

---

**Hint:**
*An easy way to remember P* x *r* x *t is to think: **"Pretty"** as in: **"Prt" simple...***

Let's do an example:

Jill receives $1000 from her grandmother on the condition that she cannot spend the money until she is 21 years old – 5 years from now. Jill decides to put that money in something called a CD (certificate of deposit) which is similar to a savings. The CD pays 10% simple interest each year. Let's calculate how much interest she gets each year and also add up the total amount she has after 5 years...

Interest for one year:

Formula:      **I = P** x **r** x **t**

Calculation:  I = $1000 x 0.1 x 1  *(Remember: 0.1 = 10%)*

              I = $100

**Hint:**
*An easy way to multiply with 10% is to simply shift the decimal point of your original amount $1,000.00 one side to the left. $1,000.00 becomes $100.00*

Once you figured out how much interest is gained in one year, you can do the same calculation five times and add up the five results.

Or you can take your yearly interest amount and multiply it by 5 which is the total number of years. That's also how the formula works in practice.

<u>Simple interest for five years:</u>

Formula:      $I = P \times r \times t$

Calculation:  $I = \$1000 \times 0.1 \times 5$

$I = \$500$

Using the formula for the entire 5 year period is obviously faster. But here is a good way to illustrate how the calculation came about and how the interest for each year has been added to the original amount Jill started with – the $1,000 from her Grandmother.

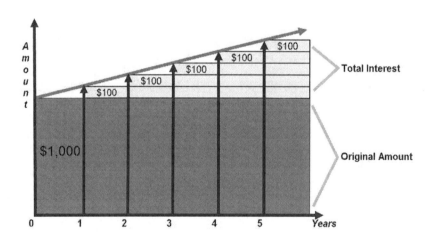

You can see how each year the same amount of interest is added to the original amount. Over time, the original balance will increase in a straight line.

<u>Let's do another example:</u>

Joe has been saving up money for the past year. He now has $400 saved up and he wants to buy the brand new iPad 2.0 which is going to be on sale six months from now. Joe wants to make sure he has these $400 available in six months so he puts all of his money into a savings account. Joe's banker tells him he can get 5% interest per year. "Great", says Joe, "let's do it". Joe deposits his $400 and six months later he shows up to get his money back and to collect his interest. On his way to the bank, he had trouble figuring out how much interest he had earned. Joe's banker helps him out explaining the calculation of simple interest again, in Joe's case when the money is invested for only a part of the year.

Remember the **"Prt simple"** interest formula?

---

**Simple Interest = P x r x t**

---

Also, remember that 5% = 0.05 and that the partial year can be calculated as a fraction. 6 months = 6/12 of a year which happens to be ½ year or 0.5 years.

We can now calculate as follows:

---

**$400 x 0.05 x 0.5 = $20 x 0.5 = $10**

---

Starting with the $400 he had saved up plus the $10 in interest for six months (half the interest of the entire year), Joe ends up with $410.

<u>One more way to check how interest works for only a partial year:</u>

Suppose Joe's beloved new iPad was available sooner than expected, say in three months' time. How much interest would he get for his $400 if the interest for his savings was again 5% per annum?

We know from before that the yearly interest was $20 which worked out as follows:

**$400 x 0.05 x 1 = $20**

We also know that three months = one quarter of a year: **3/12 = 1/4**

We can now divide the yearly interest into 4 equal pieces of $5:

**$20 ÷ 4 = $5**

If Joe had kept his $400 in the savings account for three months, he would gain an interest of $5. This is about as difficult as it gets in terms of understanding simple interest.

෭

## Compound Interest

This section is possibly the most difficult of this book in terms of using your math skills. It also happens to be one of the most important elements of modern finance. You may recall the quote at the end of the last chapter:

> *"Compound Interest is the greatest mathematical discovery of all time." - Albert Einstein*

It was indeed a remarkable discovery especially when you consider that there were no electronic calculators or spreadsheets available at the time. Given its impact throughout history, this quintessential method of accounting for interest must be considered a major factor for the expansion of mercantilism and the rise of banking during the Middle Ages leading up to the rise of today's global financial markets.

Let us take a first look at this seemingly magical formula:

$$\text{Compound interest: } P_n = P_0 (1+r)^t$$

Where,
$P_n$ = Future Value i.e. the value of your original amount + interest
$P_0$ = Present Value or Principal i.e. your original amount
$r$ = interest rate (per year)
$t$ = time (in years) a.k.a. compounding periods

OK, so this is a little more difficult to understand and to memorize. But to get you motivated to learn compound interest, let's look at a quote from another important scientist:

> *"The greatest shortcoming of the human race is our inability to understand the exponential function." - Prof. Al Bartlett*

As you saw earlier, the compound interest formula is an exponential function. It is also true that most people completely underestimate the consequences of exponential growth (one of the reasons I wrote this book by the way). We better get started then. Let's find out what compound interest and exponential growth are all about.

## What Is Compound Interest?

In the previous chapter, we learned that interest can be considered a way to make money from money or, as some say, letting your money grow. Conversely, if you have to pay interest, it is a sure way of losing money from (owing) money. Compound interest, as the name implies, just compounds everything for better or worse. It "amplifies" the simple interest, making your money grow faster but making your debt grow faster too.

In other words, compound interest occurs when you earn or pay **interest on the original amount (the principal) as well as the interest that has been accumulated.** This is unlike simple interest where the interest is always calculated on the original amount invested only.

Enough said, let's take compound interest for a test ride...

## How Compound Interest Works In Practice

Jim inherits $50,000 from his uncle and he wants to safely invest the money until he goes to college in 5 years. He will have to rely on this money to pay for most of his college expenses. Keeping that in mind, he does not want to risk any of his money and he decides to put all of it into a safe investment account. Jim's bank offers a special deal for students paying 10% per annum for a 5-year fixed deposit. A fixed deposit means Jim cannot touch that money for 5 long years. But he will enjoy higher earnings from this account based on compound interest.

So let's examine this type of investment more closely. But before we look at the more complicated compound interest formula, let's see what happens if we just calculate the interest amount for each year.

## Year 1:

We start out with $50,000 as our original amount. The interest rate is set at 10% and we can now calculate as follows:

$$\$50,000.00 \times 0.10 = \$5,000.00$$

### Remember:
*The short cut to multiply with 10% (or 0.10) is to shift the decimal point of your original amount one digit over to the left.*

You can now add the interest gained to the original amount:

> $50,000.00 +$5,000.00 =$55,000.00

**Summary: Year 1**
Starting Balance:          $50,000.00
Interest Rate: 10%
Interest during Year 1:          $5,000

Total Balance after Year 1: $55,000.00

**Year 2:**
Beginning with year 2 is where compounding starts to kick in. The amount used to calculate interest is no longer just $50,000 but it is now $55,000. You can call it the new base amount.

> $55,000.00 x 0.10 = $5,500.00

Adding the interest gained to the new base amount:

> $55,000.00 + $5,500.00 = $60,500.00

**Summary: Year 2**
New Base Amount:          $55,000.00
Interest Rate: 10%
Interest during Year 2:          $5,500.00

Total Balance after Year 2: $60,500.00

**Year 3:**
At year 3, we are also calculating interest from a new base which was the amount carried over from year 2.

> $60,500.00 x 0.10 = $6,050.00

Adding the interest gained to the new base amount:

> $60,500.00 + $6,050.00 = $66,550.00

**Summary: Year 3**

New Base Amount:          $60,500.00
Interest Rate:        10%
Interest during Year 3:       $6,050.00

Total Balance after Year 3: $66,550.00

## Year 4:

At year 4, we are again calculating interest from a new base which was the amount carried over from year 3.

$$\$66,550.00 \times 0.10 = \$6,655.00$$

Adding the interest gained to the new base amount:

$$\$66,550.00 + \$6,655.00 = \$73,205.00$$

**Summary: Year 4**

New Base Amount:          $66,550.00
Interest Rate:        10%
Interest during Year 4:       $6,655.00

Total Balance after Year 4: $73,205.00

## Year 5:

In the last period, year 5, we can do the final interest calculation based on the balance carried over from year 4.

$$\$73,205.00 \times 0.10 = \$7,320.50$$

Adding the interest gained to the new base amount:

$$\$73,205.00 + \$7,320.50 = \$80,525.50$$

**Summary: Year 5**

New Base Amount:          $73,205.00
Interest Rate: 10%
Interest during Year 5:       $7,320.50

Total Balance after Year 5: $80,525.50

To sum this up, Jim started out with the $50,000 inheritance. After 5 years of safely investing and not touching the money, his balance grew to $80,525.50, a total gain of $30,525.50. This is how compound interest was accumulated each year and how it compares to simple interest.

| Interest / Year | Compound Interest | Simple Interest |
|---|---|---|
| Interest during Year 1: | $5,000.00 | $5,000.00 |
| Interest during Year 2: | $5,500.00 | $5,000.00 |
| Interest during Year 3: | $6,050.00 | $5,000.00 |
| Interest during Year 4: | $6,655.00 | $5,000.00 |
| Interest during Year 5: | $7,320.50 | $5,000.00 |
| Total Interest: | $30,525.50 | $25,000.00 |

Putting it all together now, below is a graph showing us how each year interest was added giving us new base amounts to calculate the next year's interest amount. As you can see, one important aspect of compounding is time. The power of compounding increases, the longer you keep money invested. With each compounding period, we can amplify the interest amount, unlike simple interest, which stays the same each year no matter how many years you invest.

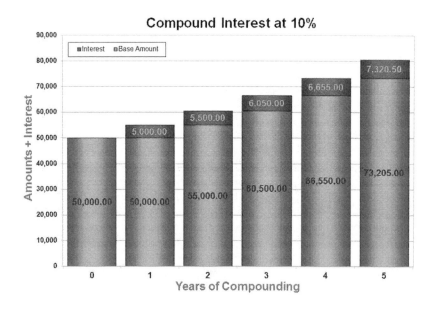

**Taking Compound Interest One Step Further**

Remember Jim from our previous example? His brother George also inherited $50,000 from his uncle. But George is a bit more adventurous and likes to take more risks. Instead of going the save route via his bank, George decides to play banker himself. He lends $50,000 to his friend Tom who just started his own online business. Tom promises to pay George 20% interest compounded annually as long as George agrees to lock-in his investment for at least 5 years. At the end of the 5 years, Tom will pay back the $50,000 plus all the interest accumulated until then. Same concept as before, so we can do this a bit faster this time just summarizing each year:

**Summary: Year 1**
Starting Balance:          $50,000.00
Interest Rate: 20%
Interest during Year 1:    $10,000.00

Total Balance after Year 1: $60,000.00

**Summary: Year 2**
Starting Balance:          $60,000.00
Interest Rate: 20%
Interest during Year 2:    $12,000.00

Total Balance after Year 2: $72,000.00

**Summary: Year 3**
Starting Balance:          $72,000.00
Interest Rate: 20%
Interest during Year 3:    $14,400.00

Total Balance after Year 3: $86,400.00

**Summary: Year 4**
Starting Balance:          $86,400.00
Interest Rate: 20%
Interest during Year 4:    $17,280.00

Total Balance after Year 4: $103,680.00

**Summary: Year 5**
Starting Balance:          $103,680.00
Interest Rate: 20%
Interest during Year 5:    $20,736.00

Total Balance after Year 5: $124,416.00

Comparing this higher compounded interest rate with simple interest makes the difference even more compelling. Within 5 years, George more than doubled his money. If he had used a simple interest method, he still would have doubled his money at 20%. But the annual compounding gave him an additional $24,416 which is almost another half of the simple interest amount over the same period.

| Interest / Year | Compound Interest | Simple Interest |
|---|---|---|
| Interest during Year 1: | $10,000.00 | $10,000.00 |
| Interest during Year 2: | $12,000.00 | $10,000.00 |
| Interest during Year 3: | $14,400.00 | $10,000.00 |
| Interest during Year 4: | $17,280.00 | $10,000.00 |
| Interest during Year 5: | $20,736.00 | $10,000.00 |
| Total Interest: | $74,416.00 | $50,000.00 |

Finally then, here is the graph putting everything together.

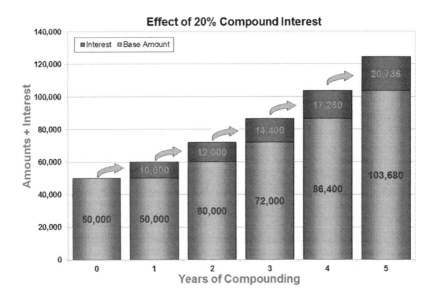

### Think About It:

*We will cover financial risk in great detail later on but here's a first look at investment risk: George is taking on a fair amount of risk by lending money to his friend instead of putting it in a bank which guarantees the amount of interest paid and that the entire amount of money plus interest will be returned at the end of 5 years.*

*A personal loan is quite different though and aside from Tom's word, George has no guarantee that he will ever get his money back, let alone make some good returns on his investment. This is one reason why a much higher interest is offered by Tom. As we will find out later in this book, the higher the risk the higher the interest or return on investment required. This is a fundamental concept in the world of finance and there are numerous expressions attesting to this concept. "No pain No gain" is one of them. You might know a few others.*

## Moving In On The Compound Interest Formula

Remember the compound interest formula we looked at a few pages back? No worries if you don't. We are now going to work out the formula together using the earlier example of Jim's $50,000 fixed deposit amount paying 10% interest compounded annually. We calculated interest in two steps but there is a more elegant way to calculate this in one step. Let me show you how to re-arrange the calculations to get to the balance plus interest.

The results will remain the same.

| Base Amount | + | Interest @ 10% |
|---|---|---|
| $50,000 | + | $50,000 x 10% |
| $50,000 x 1 | + | $50,000 x 0.10 |
| $50,000 | x | (1 + 0.10) |
| $50,000 | x | (1.10) |
| $50,000 | x | 1.10 |

Basically, adding 10% interest is the same as multiplying by 1.10

The same holds true for each additional year:

- Year 2 Base Amount + Interest: $55,000 x 1.10 = $60,500.00
- Year 3 Base Amount + Interest: $60,500 x 1.10 = $66,550.00
- Year 4 Base Amount + Interest: $66,550 x 1.10 = $73,205.00
- Year 5 Base Amount + Interest: $73,205 x 1.10 = $80,525.50

This lengthy process can be simplified if we calculate right from the start all the way to Year 5 by multiplying 5 times:

$$\$50,000 \times 1.10 \times 1.10 \times 1.10 \times 1.10 \times 1.10 = \$80,525.50$$

We can now simplify further by converting this series of equal multiples to exponents. It is the same concept as $3 \times 3 = (3)^2$.

Therefore: $1.10 \times 1.10 \times 1.10 \times 1.10 \times 1.10 = (1.10)^5$

and the formula reverts to: $50,000 \times (1.10)^5 = \$80,525.50$

As a final step, we can rewrite $(1.10)^5 = (1+0.10)^5$

And voila, here is our compound interest formula again:

**Compound Interest = $\$50,000\ (1+0.10)^5$**

### Yet More About Compounding

As you might have guessed, there are variations of interest terms as well as compounding terms. We will discuss the more complex variations of interest in the coming chapters. The summary below gives you a nice overview of what we learned in this chapter along with a preview of things to come.

Simple Interest:

Formula:     $P \times r \times t$
Features:    Fixed return each year; interest remains the same
Example:    Bond coupon payments

Annual Compounding:

Formula:     $P \times (1+r)^t$
Features:    Interest amount changes each year; return grows
Example:    Savings Accounts, CDs

Monthly Compounding:

Formula:     $P \times (1+r/n)^{t \times n}$
Features:    Interest amount changes each month; return grows
Example:    Mortgages

# Time Value of Money

If someone offered to pay you $100 today or the same amount one year from now which one would you pick?

Most certainly you would take the $100 today but why is that?

Something called inflation is usually causing the prices of the things we buy to rise over time. Talk to your grandparents and they might tell you that in their days, they could buy lunch for only 50 cents. Today, you might be hard pressed to buy anything other than chewing gum for the same amount.

Your hard earned cash tends to lose buying power over time; that is you can buy less with the same amount of money. To counter that, you could invest the $100 received today and make some more money within a year's time. That is where our previous chapter on interest comes in handy.

This is really one of those big dilemmas in the world of finance because you have to make a choice between something of value (your cash) for another thing called time. You can't have both at once. You either get the money now and spend it or you save your money and spend it later. If you wait and spend it later you want your money to grow over time and be rewarded for not spending it right now. Otherwise, why bother waiting knowing that your dollars will buy you less over time. Can you see that time has value?

The same thought process is the basis for this fundamental concept of finance called the time value of money. The time value of money is really at the heart of most financial products from the basic savings account to the most complex derivatives. No worries, we will learn more about investing later in this book and discuss the most important types of investments in detail. For now, it is important to remember that time is an important factor with all things financial.

> ### *Think About It:*
> *Here is an easy way to figure out why time is so crucially important when it comes to finance. Remember the "**Prt**" simple formula for simple interest? t = time and without the "t" in that formula, or in any other interest formula for that matter, you would only be able to account for the current interest, in other words never look beyond one year.*
>
> *As a musician, can you imagine music without time? Where does it start and where does it end? Can you capture and appreciate music without any reference for time? Would you be able to play with other musicians?*

## Variations Of Interest

So far we discussed two of the most common types of interest: Simple interest and compound interest. As luck would have it, there are numerous variations of how interest can be calculated. Again, a crucial factor in these calculations is time, in particular how time is accounted for.

## Interest Calculations For Certain Number Of Days

Our previous calculations assumed that we calculate the interest for one entire year. We also examined how a partial year i.e. three months or six months could easily be derived by dividing the interest for the entire year into equal parts using a pie chart. One year has 12 months hence, the interest for only 6 months would be 6/12 or one half of the entire year's interest.

In practice however, you don't always keep your money invested for exactly one, two, three complete months or years. You might put some of your money into a savings account but you may need the money in say 150 days exactly. In that case, we would need to calculate the interest for the partial year counting the number of days. This is actually much easier than it sounds. You can intuitively figure out the interest for only part of the year with this example:

Paula received $1000 from her grandparents as a Christmas present and a combined contribution to help her pay for the next summer vacation. She wants to go to a summer camp in Italy in July. Until then, she wants to keep the money tucked away safely but also wants to gain a bit of interest in the meantime. Paula's mom suggests opening a savings account where Paula can receive 4% interest per annum. Let us calculate how much interest she can get if she opens the account after Christmas and keeps the money in the account for exactly 150 days.

Let us calculate the interest amount for the entire year first with our **"Prt"** **simple** interest formula:

> Formula for calculating simple interest: $I = P \times r \times t$

In this case: **$1,000 x 0.04 x 1 = $40**

$40 is the interest gained for the entire year. Therefore, the interest for only 150 days of the year must be smaller. It would actually be a fraction of the entire year. We know there are 365 days in a year. If the entire year gives us an interest of $40, how much can we get for only 150 days? This sounds like an easy math problem you may remember from pre-Algebra but we don't want to confuse you with equations solving for "x".

Instead think about it this way. If you can get $40 for the entire 365 days, then you must get $40/365 of interest for one day only.

Using a calculator: $40 / 365 = $0.1095890 which rounds to $0.11.

So you get 11 cents of interest per day. This means for 150 days, you will get 150 x $0.11 = $16.50 in interest.

What we just did is to substitute the entire year time period for the exact number of days in a year:

$$t = 150/365$$

We can now convert our "**Prt**" **simple** formula to easily calculate interest for any number of days within a year.

$$I = P \times r \times \frac{\text{#of days}}{365}$$

## The Banker's Rule

Using the exact number of days in a year gives us the correct interest gained on any investment held for a certain number of days within a year. But as you can see from the above formula, it isn't something you can easily calculate in your head. You may be surprised, but bankers are actually not that good at calculating especially if they don't have a calculator at hand. To simplify things, the bankers came up with a solution that makes the calculations, particularly for loans much easier. They just assume that each year has only 360 days when interest is counted. That translates into 30 days for each month. Our formula now looks like this:

$$I = P \times r \times \frac{\text{#of days}}{360}$$

With this method, the calculations can be done a lot easier essentially using fractions of 12 so that you can roughly figure out some of these calculations in your head.

For instance, if you had $1,000 invested for 90 days paying you 4% interest each year, you can derive the interest amount quite easily without a calculator.

- 4% interest on $1,000 gives you $40 per year
- 90 days are 90/360 or 9/36 = 1/4
- 1/4 of $40 = $10

This method makes it easy, even for the bankers who aren't that good at mental math.

In a later chapter, we will discuss some special compound interest calculations where interest is compounded monthly instead of yearly. Those methods are used when you buy a home and get a loan from a bank to finance part of the purchase. A loan like that is called a mortgage.

Again, the use of 360 days of counting interest makes a lot of sense in simplifying the math for these calculations. Because the bankers came up with this idea, it is also called the **Banker's Rule** and it is common practice for interest calculations in many countries.

### Finance Trivia:
*Most European countries as well as the United States us the 360-day method for calculating interest. The United Kingdom and Japan use a 365 days per to calculate interest. A few financial offerings even use 366 days in a leap year.*

ଚ୨

## Accrued Interest

This seems like a good time to introduce another financial term:

### Accrued Interest

Accrued interest is really just a fancy word for interest accumulated or gained but not yet received. Accrued interest comes into play when you have money invested over a certain period of time for instance, in a fixed deposit account. In a one-year fixed account, interest is compounded annually and the amount of interest is paid by the bank at the end of the year. That means you don't see that interest money until a few days after the year ended when you receive your bank account statement. Technically however, the bank owes you interest for every single day that you put your money in that savings account; they just don't have to pay you until the year is complete.

The example on the graph below shows $1,000 earning 10% interest. You can see how interest is accrued during the year but is only paid to your account at the end of the year. If you fixed deposit account for say 240 days, the bank would have to pay you $66.67 in interest. Along with your original balance of $1,000 the bank would have to pay you $1,066.67 for your 8-month deposit period.

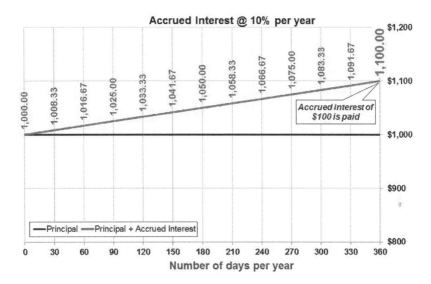

### Think About It:
When devising the terms of some complex financial instruments known as derivatives, investment banks often use 365.25 days per year to calculate interest. Can you guess why?

## The Nerd Corner
For the nerds among you, check out how you can modify our simple interest formula with just a bit of basic algebra:

<u>Variations of the simple interest formula</u>

Solving for time:

$$t = I / P \times r$$

Solving for interest rate:

$$r = I / P \times t$$

Solving for principal value:

$$P = I / r \times t$$

☜☞

# The Rule of 72

In the previous chapters, we spent quite a bit of time on simple and compound interest. We can easily remember the formula for simple interest which was **"Prt" simple**.

Compound interest however, was a bit more "iffy." What was that formula again? Could you pull that off if someone asked you on the street?

Perhaps you will remember, but just in case you don't, there are ways to estimate how compound interest can affect your money over time. We will show you a short cut that is very easy to learn but still very effective in finding a close approximation for compound interest. It is so easy you won't even need a calculator.

The **Rule of 72** is a simplified way to determine how long an investment will take to double, given a fixed compound interest rate.

☜☞

# Einstein's Advice

We quoted Albert Einstein previously as he referred to compound interest as "the greatest mathematical discovery of all time".

Albert Einstein loved the Rule of 72 and he acknowledged it as an ingenious way to quickly estimate how many years it takes to double your money at a given interest rate. So if you can remember Einstein's famous formula $E = mc^2$ you should be able to remember this:

---

**72 ÷ interest rate =  # of years it takes to double your money**

---

Let's do an example:

Betty puts $10,000 in an investment that pays a return of 10% compound interest per year. How many years will it take to double that amount and grow the investment to $20,000?

Based on the rule of 72, we would calculate as follows:

**72 ÷ 10 (%) = 7.2 (years)**

Solution:   $10,000 invested with a return of 10% compound interest will take 7.2 years to grow to $20,000.

Remember, this formula is an approximation not 100% accurate, but pretty close. If you'd like to calculate numbers to the nearest cent, here's a reminder of our compound interest formula:

---

Compound interest:  $P_n = P_0 (1+r)^t$

---

Where,
$P_n$ = Future Value i.e. the value of your original amount + interest
$P_0$ = Present Value or Principal i.e. your original amount
$r$  = interest rate (per year)
$t$  = time (in years) a.k.a. compounding periods

The Rule of 72 also works to find out the interest rate you need if you wanted to double your money within a certain number of years. You can rework the Rule of 72 like this:

---

**72 ÷ # of years =  the rate needed to double your money**

---

Here is an example:

Mark has $5,000 saved up. He is eager to double that amount in the next 6 years but he is not sure what type of investment or interest would be needed to achieve that goal.  Let's plug in the numbers.

**72 ÷ 6 (years) = 12 (%)**

Solution: In order to double $5,000 in 6 years' time, Mark will need to find an investment giving him a compounded rate of return of 12%.

---

### Reality Check:

*The interest rates and percentages we have used in our examples so far are a bit on the high side when it comes to the investing returns. During periods of economic stagnation and in times of recessions, interest rates can be very low. Some of our assumptions for investment returns have to be looked at with a grain of salt. But the main purpose of the seemingly high rates of return is to make the comparisons and examples easy to grasp.*

*For example, when you examine the rates of loans, foremost the credit card financing rates, you will notice that those rates are always a lot higher than savings rates. That difference is even more evident when the general interest rates are at record lows, as was the case during the Great Recession of 2008-2009. With record low interest rates, you might get only as much as 1% interest on your savings whereas credit cards usually have financing rates of 20% or more - quite a difference.*

***This leads us to an important revelation when it comes to finance. Without exception, the financial institutions that hold "YOUR MONEY", i.e. your bank or your broker, create terms that work in their favor rather than in yours. Therefore, the interest you receive on your savings will never be anywhere as high as the rates charged for a loan. The difference between receiving and paying interest from the bank's point of view is easy profit. Sadly, that is not something the banks are willing to give up for your sake.***

*It is therefore immensely important that you always read and understand the terms and conditions your bank is offering for their services. You too do <u>not</u> want to give up part of your money so that banks can make even bigger profits.*

---

### Approximate Versus Exact Calculations

We noted earlier that the Rule of 72 is an approximation to figure out the number of years it takes to double your investment at a given interest rate. The inquiring mind might ask, how good an approximation is that rule actually? Well, there is no single answer for that question because the accuracy changes depending on the interest rate. The Rule of 72 is extremely accurate in the range between 5% and 15%. At much lower or much higher rates, the accuracy fades and the Rule turns more into an approximation.

The table below lists the doubling times (in years) for the exact calculation as well as the approximation via the Rule of 72.

| Interest Rate | Exact Calculation | Rule of 72 | Difference |
|---------------|-------------------|------------|------------|
| 0.5% | 138.98 | 144.00 | 5.02 |
| 1% | 69.66 | 72.00 | 2.34 |
| 2% | 35.00 | 36.00 | 1.00 |
| 3% | 23.45 | 24.00 | 0.55 |
| 4% | 17.67 | 18.00 | 0.33 |
| 5% | 14.21 | 14.40 | 0.19 |
| 6% | 11.90 | 12.00 | 0.10 |
| 7% | 10.25 | 10.29 | 0.04 |
| 8% | 9.01 | 9.00 | -0.01 |
| 9% | 8.04 | 8.00 | -0.04 |
| 10% | 7.27 | 7.20 | -0.07 |
| 11% | 6.64 | 6.55 | -0.10 |
| 12% | 6.12 | 6.00 | -0.12 |
| 15% | 4.96 | 4.80 | -0.16 |
| 20% | 3.80 | 3.60 | -0.20 |
| 25% | 3.11 | 2.88 | -0.23 |
| 50% | 1.71 | 1.44 | -0.27 |
| 100% | 1.00 | 0.72 | -0.28 |

**Think About It:**
You can see from the table that the Rule of 72 works great between 5% and 15%; the numbers are very close to the actual calculation. That is not the case for extremely low and extremely high rates though. When dealing with very low and even more so with very high interest rates, it is a good idea to calculate the exact number of years with our compound interest formula. Remember that a little bit of extra work in getting higher accuracy can pay off with more Dollars in your pocket instead of more Dollars in your banker's pocket.

# The Guitar Player's Rule Of 72

If you are a guitar player, the number 72 should ring a bell. In case it doesn't, let's take a look at something that most musicians, certainly every guitar player should recognize immediately:

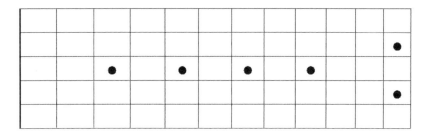

You guessed it – an image of a guitar fret board. 72 still doesn't ring a bell? Well here we go...

There are 6 strings and 12 frets (the traditional range where most of the guitar playing activity takes place). 6 x 12 = 72.

Next time you wonder what that number was that allowed you to quickly calculate the doubling times for investing your money, think of the guitar and **6** strings multiplied by **12** frets = **72** notes.

Here's the Rule of 72 one more time:

**72 ÷ interest rate = # of years it takes to double your money**

∽

# Cousins Of The Rule Of 72

Let's meet the cousins of the Rule of 72, namely the **Rule of 114** and the **Rule of 144**. Since all three rules belong to the same family, they all provide an approximation to calculate some scenarios for compound interest.

The Rule of 114 approximates the number of years it takes to triple your money. This is the formula:

> **114 ÷ interest rate =  # of years needed to triple your money**

Let's do an example:

Paula puts $10,000 in an investment that pays a return of 6% compound interest per year. How many years will it take to triple that amount and grow the investment to $30,000?

Based on the rule of 114, we calculate as follows:

$$114 \div 6 = 19$$

Solution: $10,000 invested with a return of 6% compound interest will take 19 years to grow to $30,000.

Lastly, let's meet the Rule of 144 which allows you to easily calculate the number of years it takes to quadruple your money. Here is the formula:

> **144 ÷ interest rate = # of years to quadruple your money**

<u>For example:</u>

Monica puts $10,000 in an investment that pays a return of 9% compound interest per year. How many years will it take to quadruple that amount and grow the investment to $40,000?

Based on the rule of 144, we calculate as follows:

$$144 \div 9 = 16$$

Solution: $10,000 invested with a return of 9% compound interest will take 16 years to grow to $40,000.

# THREE

## *All About Banking*

### From Piggy Banks to Real Banks

Having learned the history of money and banking earlier, we are now ready to take a closer look at how banks operate today and learn about the various types of services banks have on offer.

When you boil things down to basics, a bank could be looked at like a giant Piggy Bank. Most of us grew up with a Piggy Bank putting in our pennies, nickels, dimes, quarters and on occasion, a few dollar bills too. Every once in a while, we would pick up the piggy bank, get a sense of how heavy or how full it is, shake it a bit to make sure those coins are still there. The Piggy Bank then was there for a purpose; that is to save some money maybe to buy a new toy or something we always wanted. But it was also a safe place to put your money, since it was closed off all around, you could only put money into it. As a child, you must have felt that the Piggy Bank was a safe place to put your money.

The concept of putting your money into a safe place is the same with a real bank too. You can bring your money to the bank and the bank is supposed to keep it safe. To let you know that the money is still there, the bank issues a bank statement, usually once a month. The bank statement is your receipt for giving your money to the bank. The Bank statement also shows additional details all of which will be covered in the coming pages.

We are also going to learn about the different types of bank accounts you can have as well as how to open an account and how to best manage your bank account(s).

∽

## Types of Bank Accounts

The two most common types of bank accounts are checking accounts and savings accounts. We will cover both of them in detail. There are many other types of accounts as well. We are now going to learn about the different types of bank accounts and banking services.

### Checking Accounts

A checking account is an account that is linked to a check book. This account gives you the ability to write a check which is said to draw funds from your checking account.

## What is a check?

A check is a piece of paper that shows how much money is paid to some-one by the writer of the check. We will learn more about checks, how to write a check and how to properly use checks and checking accounts in a following chapter.

> ### *Think About It:*
> *Checks are the modern versions of "bills of exchange." Remember, they first appeared in the early days of banking during the Middle Ages and were created to make payments without the need to carry around heavy gold and silver bullion. Today's paper money also evolved from these bills of exchange for the same reasons - convenience and efficiency. Can you see the similarities between checks and paper money (i.e. your Dollars)? What do you think are the differences between paying with a check as opposed to paying with Dollar bills?*

Example of a checking account:

Joe has a checking account with First Musician's Bank. He opened that account just last week when he deposited $1,000 with that bank. His checking account therefore has a balance of $1,000 and Joe decides to write his first check when he is at the local music store buying new strings for his bass guitar. The strings cost $25 including tax. Joe writes out his first check to the name of the local music store in the amount of $25.

The music store gets paid when Joe's check is cleared through the music store's bank account.

Checking accounts have been around for a long time. They offer a convenient way to pay for your usual bills, groceries and other expenses you might have.

Most banks actually offer numerous types of checking accounts with different features and also different charges. When opening a bank account it is a good idea to find the account that suits your needs best. However, most banks offer a basic checking account which usually gives you a good range of services for free. Remember, we are trying to manage our finances and if we can avoid an expense, even if it's just a few dollars, we should do so. In case your banker is telling you they don't offer any free checking accounts, you should consider changing your bank.

# Savings Accounts

The traditional savings accounts were also called passbook savings accounts. When you opened a traditional savings account you received a little book that looked almost like a passport. The book was filled with pages where your bank would keep a record of your deposits and withdrawals as well as your latest balance. As recently as the 1980's, customers had to go to the bank at least once a year, if they wanted the interest on their savings account recorded in the passbook. Of course the bank also kept internal records of what these balances were for each customer. However, the passbook was essentially a receipt and statement for the transactions that happened in a savings account.

A few years earlier in the 1970's some bank entries were still hand-written and the bank teller had to put a stamp and his signature with each new entry to confirm that it was the bank, not someone else making the entries in your savings book.

Today, there are many types of savings accounts with slightly different terms and, of course, varying degrees of interest offered. As a general rule, banks give better interest rates for higher minimum deposits. If you opened a savings account with $25,000 your interest rate might be 0.5% higher than say an account with only $1,000. Your rates will also be higher if you promise not to withdraw any money for a certain time period. We will learn more about these types of accounts next.

### Fixed Deposit/Time Deposit Account
A special type of savings account is called a fixed deposit or time deposit account. This type of account is held for a certain fixed or minimum length of time. Unlike a standard savings account which could be opened today and closed the next day, fixed deposit accounts have to be kept for a minimum period of time. Depending on the bank and type of deposit, this could range anywhere from one week to 5 years. Banks offer higher interest rates on longer deposits and you might know why that is. Remember the concept of the *Time Value of Money*? In order to get a higher rate, you have to forego spending the money now. From the bank's point of view, the bank is prepared to pay you higher rates for the privilege of using your money for a longer period of time.

### Certificate of Deposit (CD)
No, not the compact discs you may find in your parents' music collection, a CD is also a type of savings account. Some people also call it a savings certificate.

CD's have a fixed end date called a maturity date as well as a fixed interest rate. This means, you cannot hold a CD as long as you want. The bank offering the CD sets the time frame, say 2 years from now when the CD is said to "mature". At that point in time, the buyer of the CD will be paid back the original deposit plus interest earned.

Similar to fixed deposit accounts, the longer you keep your money in a CD, the higher the interest rate. Again, we see how the concept of **Time Value of Money** determines your financial reward.

CDs are offered anywhere from 1 month to 10 years and most CDs are insured by the **FDIC** (see chapter on history of banking) which makes them a very secure type of investment.

### *Think About It:*

*CD's and fixed deposit accounts lock in your money for a certain period of time. In a way, that is a good thing because it forces you to stick with your (savings) plan and wait before spending your money. But you are also rewarded for your patience with a higher interest rate in the end. Although the term is fixed, it is still possible to withdraw your money prior to the maturity date. However, you will have to go through some extra paperwork and you might also have to pay a penalty. This is called an early withdrawal penalty.*

*Can you appreciate the rationale for a penalty in this case? Could this also have to do with the time value of money? Put yourself in the shoes of the bank and think about the consequence of a client wanting to withdraw his money early. The bank which usually invests your money somewhere else is now forced to pay you, the client, earlier than expected. The bank might have to borrow the same amount elsewhere and someone has to make up the difference in lost interest in the end. From the banker's perspective that is reasonable and in the best case scenario for you, the owner of the CD, the penalty would be roughly the difference in interest that was lost due to your early withdrawal. But more often than not, bankers also charge for the inconvenience, additional administrative costs etc. Therefore, it is a good idea to carefully plan ahead and minimize the chances of being penalized with additional fees. As you may have guessed by now, the time value of money affects these penalty fees too.*

Let us run through an example of a typical CD investment:

Say you bought a $10,000 CD with an interest rate of 4.8% per annum and a term of one year until the CD ends. At the end of the year, the CD will have grown to $10,480.  Since this is just a one year CD we won't need to use compound interest but we can use **"Prt" simple** interest formula to calculate the interest:

$$I = P \times r \times t$$

**I** = **$10,000** × **0.048** × 1 = **$480**

**$10,000** (initial investment) + **$480** (earned interest) = **$10,480**

Exercise:
Suppose you had bought the $10,000 CD above and everything works fine until you run into a problem. One month before the CD matures, there is an emergency and you need the cash to pay for some medical bills. Although this is not typically the case, your friendly banker gives you a break because of your emergency situation. He agrees to only charge you the lost interest, no other penalties. Let us calculate how much money you would get back after withdrawing one month early.

Interest earned for the entire year = $480

Interest for 1 month per year = $480 / 12 = $40

Interest for 11 months per year = $40 x 11 = **$440**

In this case then, the entire amount of accrued interest until month 11 has been paid and the CD returned the fair amount of interest for the given time period.  Please remember though, most banks will charge penalties on top of lost interest.  Often, you end up with somewhat less than the original amount invested, especially if you terminate the CD within the first few months. That happens when the fees alone are higher than the accrued interest until then.

**Money Market Accounts**
A Money Market Account a.k.a. "Money Market Deposit Account" is a special type of savings account. It offers slightly higher interest rates than a regular savings account but it needs certain minimum deposits to open the account.

There are also some restrictions on the account. Some of the restrictions include that you might only be able to do five transactions in a month.

Some banks require at least $1,000 to open this kind of account. However, the restrictions and minimum account opening deposits can vary from bank to bank. As always, it pays to shop around and compare the rates and services offered.

## Hybrid Accounts

You may have heard of "Hybrid Cars" that run on gasoline but also partially on electricity. In Banking, there are so-called hybrid accounts and they have been around long before hybrid cars were invented. As the name implies, a hybrid account is a mix between two types of accounts.

A good example might be a combination of a traditional savings account and a checking account. That kind of savings account allows you to write checks on the account. The advantage of this kind of account is that it combines the convenience of a checking account with the higher interest rate of a savings account.

There are also so many types of services, often automated to give more convenience and security to bank customers. Some banks offer a link between checking and savings accounts and you can setup so-called standing instructions on the account. Standing instructions are automated services. For instance, you can automatically transfer any amount over say $1,000 from your checking account to your savings account. This way, you can take advantage of slightly higher interest rates in your savings account.

A practical example:

Joan works for a newspaper. Every month, the newspaper deposits Joan's pay check into her checking account. After paying taxes and other deductions, Joan has a net salary of $3,250 each month. Joan has to pay for certain expenses such as rent, insurance, utilities etc. which usually ads up to about $2,000 each month. She likes to keep a minimum balance of at least $1,000 in her checking account. Her savings account gives her about 3% interest while she gets no interest on her checking account. Anytime she has some extra money left, she tries to shift as much as possible over to her savings account to maximize the interest benefit she gets.

Her bank allows her to setup an automated service and after all her expenses are paid, any amount above $1,000 is automatically transferred over to the savings account. In this case, the bank transfers $250 from Joan's checking account to her savings account. Although Joan could do this by herself, the automated service never forgets. It is a convenient way for her to manage her finances better and to not let go of a bit of additional interest income.

**Think About It:**
*Can you think of other ways to automate certain banking services? What would be your priority list of services a bank should offer to make you want to do business with them?*

## Online Banking

It was not too long ago when savers had to step inside a bank to record the accrued interest of one year's worth of savings in the savings pass book. Today, everything is of course recorded electronically and banks offer access to almost all types of accounts via the Internet. Account statements can still be mailed to your home but all account activity such as transactions, deposits, withdrawals, interest given, fees deducted, etc., are available via online banking.

Whether you do your transactions online or the traditional way by receiving banks statements through the mail and by visiting your bank's local branch, the basic services of your bank should be available either way.

**Think About It:**
*Today, there are just a few banks offering online-only banking services. In exchange for giving up something i.e. the access to a local branch, online banks can sometimes offer slightly better terms than a traditional bank.*

*When we learned about the history of banking, we asked whether traditional bank notes and coins might one day disappear because electronic money (credit, debit cards) are more convenient.*

*Along the same lines of thinking, can you envision a future wherein local bank branches disappear altogether and banking will be limited to telephone and online services? If cash and coins were to disappear, why would you really need a bank branch? And how about ATMs, could they disappear because of the same reason?*

## Banking for Teenagers & Kids

If you are under 18, banks only offer a few bank account choices. The most common accounts for kids are savings accounts. Some banks offer joint accounts with parents to help teenagers learn about the use of bank accounts and to get them ready for college and work. All other banking services have to wait until you are of legal age.

## Comparing Bank Accounts

Among the many types, we looked at six main forms of bank accounts. Let us now summarize the main features as well as the pros and cons of each of these accounts.

### Checking Account

| | |
|---|---|
| Earns Interest: | no |
| Account Fees: | yes/no |
| Access money anytime: | yes |
| Check writing allowed: | yes |
| Transfers to other accounts: | yes |
| FDIC insured: | yes |

### CDs or Fixed Deposit Account

| | |
|---|---|
| Earns Interest: | yes |
| Account Fees: | no |
| Access money anytime: | yes |
| Check writing allowed: | limited |
| Transfers to other accounts: | yes |
| FDIC insured: | yes |

### Money Market Account

| | |
|---|---|
| Earns Interest: | yes |
| Account Fees: | yes/no |
| Access money anytime: | yes |
| Check writing allowed: | limited |
| Transfers to other accounts: | limited |
| FDIC insured: | yes |

### Hybrid/Special Account

| | |
|---|---|
| Earns Interest: | yes/no |
| Account Fees: | yes/no |
| Access money anytime: | yes |
| Check writing allowed: | yes |
| Transfers to other accounts: | yes |
| FDIC insured: | yes |

# How To Open A Bank Account

Today, most banks offer at least a dozen different types of accounts. That can make it a bit tricky to figure out exactly what combination of accounts might work best for you. In case you are opening your first bank account on your own, a basic checking and basic savings account should normally be sufficient for most of your banking needs. You should also make sure that both accounts can be managed online. It's just more convenient that way.

## Documents needed to open a bank account
Banks have been making the account opening process quite easy these days. Still, there are a number of documents required before you can open a bank account.

### 1. Social Security Number
Banks have to ask for your Social Security Number to verify your identity and perform a credit check before processing an account application.

### 2. Identification
Your driver's license, I.D. or passports are acceptable forms of photo identification. Some banks also require a second form of ID which could be in the form of a credit card or a birth certificate.

### 3. Completed Account Application
The account application will ask you to fill in your name, birth date, current address, citizenship and some other personal information.

෨

# All About Checks

We just learned that a check is a piece of paper that specifies a payment of money from one person to another. The person writing the check is called the **drawer** or **writer** of the check. The person or company receiving the check is called the **payee.**

Let us look at a typical payment by check:

Meet Chris, the drummer. Chris is still in college but he has been doing paper rounds for a whole year and has managed to save enough money to buy a drum set. He finds a very nice used drum set on Craigslist. After calling up the seller and agreeing on a time to meet, Chris can try out the drums and negotiate the final price. All works out as planned for Chris; he likes the drum set and the price is okay too. Tom, the seller of the drums, wants $750. Chris brought his checkbook and is ready to write the check. He is writing the check in the name of Tom. Tom can now take this check to his bank and deposit the check into his checking account. The bank arranges with Chris' bank so that the correct amount is deducted from Chris' checking account and transferred to Tom's checking account. When this happens, the check has been cleared.

<u>The graphic below shows us how Chris paid for his drum set:</u>

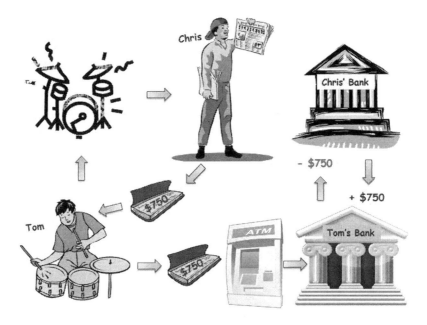

### Understanding Your Check
Before writing your first check you should take a minute to examine what the sections and numbers on a check mean.

1) Your name and address is usually printed on the top left-hand corner of the check. When paying someone with a check, the payee often requires you to show your driver's license or ID. Confirming that the name and address match with your ID is a good way to verify that the person is giving you a good check. More on this when we talk about how to keep all your financial assets safe.

2) Your bank assigns a unique number for each check that is printed. The check number shows up in two places: top right-hand corner and at the bottom of the check.

3) Each check has three sets of numbers printed at the bottom. The first set of numbers shows the bank routing number. Each bank has a unique routing number which is needed to identify the bank so that the check can be cleared through the banking system.

4) Your checking account number is printed on the check as well. This is also needed to clear the check through the banking system. Once the bank is identified, the account number tells the banking system which

account to deduct the money from. Today, check clearing happens electronically; a machine reads the numbers at the bottom of the check as well as the amount specified.

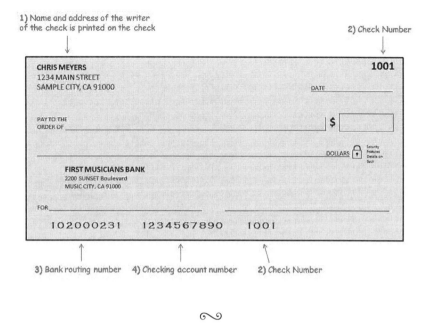

1) Name and address of the writer of the check is printed on the check

2) Check Number

3) Bank routing number  4) Checking account number  2) Check Number

## Writing Your First Check

Now that we know the basic elements of a blank check, we can write our first check.

5) Write the name of the person or company you wish to pay on the line next to "PAY TO THE ORDER OF".

6) You have to write the amount in words, for example "Seven hundred fifty". When your amount includes cents, you also have to write out the cents as a fraction of 100.  For instance, if the amount was $750.20 you would write "Seven hundred fifty and $^{20}/_{100}$".

7) Always remember to write the correct date on your check.  Nobody will accept your check if the date is missing.

8) You can write a personal memo or reference as a reason for the payment.  When making payments to some companies for electricity, gas or your phone company, they ask you to write down your payment or invoice numbers for the bill you are paying. This helps them to properly record your payment.

9) Make sure you sign the check. It is also important that you use the same signature that is on file with your bank. Although banks only spot

check if a signature is correct, you should remember that your own personal signature is also a piece of identification for the bank. Your signature is in place for your security since only you know how to sign exactly that same way.

10) Last but not least, the payment amount has to be written in the box provided. This time you have to use numbers for the dollars and cents and of course, those numbers have to match the amount you wrote in words on the line six earlier.

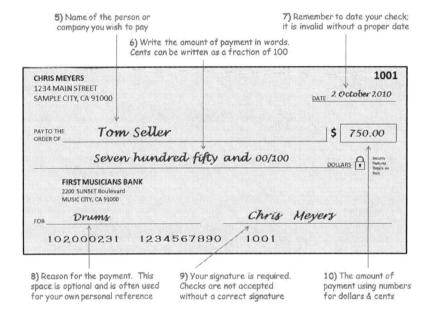

5) Name of the person or company you wish to pay

6) Write the amount of payment in words. Cents can be written as a fraction of 100

7) Remember to date your check; it is invalid without a proper date

8) Reason for the payment. This space is optional and is often used for your own personal reference

9) Your signature is required. Checks are not accepted without a correct signature

10) The amount of payment using numbers for dollars & cents

## Think About It:
*Can you see why the signature is just one of the many security features built in to a check and its check clearing process? Can you list all the security elements that need to be in place so that the payment can make its way from your checking account - via your checkbook - to the payee's checking account?*

### Writing Numbers In Words
Have you considered some of the security features of checks? One of the first things you should do when receiving a check is to make sure that all necessary entries are filled in.

Next, do a simple spot check to compare the amount written in words with the amount written in numbers inside the box next to the Dollar sign.

Both entries have to match or else the check is not accepted. This is a simple but very effective deterrent making it more difficult for a thief to change the amount on your check in case he was trying to gain an extra advantage.

Imagine the $750 Tom just received from Chris; it would be easy to add one or two zeroes to the amount of $750. However, those extra zeros no longer match with the amount written in words. **Seven hundred fifty** is completely different from **$7,500** which is written **"seven thousand five hundred"**.

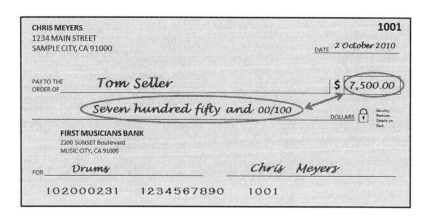

## Basic Rules For Writing Numbers In Words

**1.** Make sure the amount in words matches the amount in numbers.

**2.** Numbers between 20 and 100 are hyphenated – exceptions are the numbers 20, 30, 40, etc.

- **25 => Twenty-five**
- **36 => Thirty-six**
- **77 => Seventy-seven**

**3.** Only use the word "and" in place of the decimal point. As we learned earlier, the cents are written as a fraction of 100. Reason being, 100 cents equal 1 Dollar.

- **$17.50**    **=> Seventeen and $^{50}/_{100}$**
- **$365.25**    **=> Three hundred sixty-five and $^{25}/_{100}$**
- **$2,300.78**   **=> Two thousand three hundred and $^{78}/_{100}$**

**4.** When you have full dollar amounts (without cents) you can write the section for cents in a number of ways:

a)    $75 => **Seventy-five and $^{00}/_{100}$**
b)    $75 => **Seventy-five and $^{no}/_{100}$**
c)    $75 => **Seventy-five and $^{xx}/_{100}$**
d)    $75 => **Seventy-five only**

### Practice What You Just Learned
Writing your first check can be a bit overwhelming. There are so many things to consider and to make sure everything is completed just right. That is why you should practice writing numbers and writing checks.

### When You Get Paid With A Check
Let's say you and your friends want to see a concert. You volunteer to purchase the tickets in advance to get a group discount. When the tickets finally arrive via mail, you call your friends and tell them to come over to pick up the tickets. One of your friends doesn't bring enough cash but he brought his checkbook along. He writes a check in your name for $20 and you hand over the concert ticket. You have the check now, what happens next?

Earlier, we learned what happens when Tom Seller deposits his check to his bank. Let us now take a closer look at what it takes to get your hands on the cash.

### Check the Check Before You Deposit
When you receive a check, verify all necessary details first before even thinking of depositing that check. As we learned earlier, you need to make sure that the following info is correctly completed:

- Your name appears and is spelled correctly.

- The check is properly dated; current date is preferred.

- Payment amount written in numbers inside the box next to the Dollar sign has to match the amount written in words.

- Verify that the check is signed.

- Verify the name & address of the person by checking his/her I.D.

Verifying the name and ID of a friend will not be necessary but it is highly recommended when you receive a check from someone you don't know that well. If a stranger gives you a check, be extra careful and double check all information. It won't hurt to play it safe!

**_Think About It:_**
_Having the current date on a check is important because it is a requirement of any legal contract to assign an effective date. The date on the check effectively makes this legal contract enforceable. If someone gave you a check and wrote the date correct but entered the next year instead of the current year it would be considered a **post-dated check**. Would you accept a post-dated check? What kinds of problems could you be facing if someone gave you a post-dated check?_

## How To Deposit Checks

When you bring you check to the bank, you also have to complete a deposit slip along with your check. The deposit slip provides the bank the necessary information to credit the right account, namely your account.

Let us practice how to complete a deposit slip. Imagine you were Tom Seller, the person from our previous example who sold his drum set to Chris. Tom has Chris' check for $750 in his hands and he is ready to deposit that check with his bank. At his bank, the teller gives him a deposit slip and shows him how to complete it. Tom has to fill in the following details:

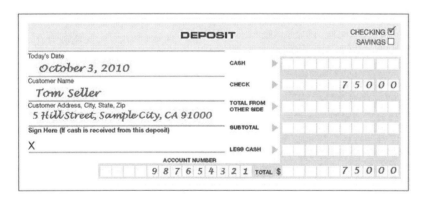

As you can see, this is quite simple: Enter today's date, your name and address, but also let the bank know where you want this money to be deposited. Most people deposit checks into their checking account. However, you can tell the bank to deposit it into your savings account too. Once the check is cleared, the money is then deposited to the account number you specified on the deposit slip.

**Banker's Jargon:**
When Tom makes the $750 check deposit at his bank, Bankers say they **credit** Tom's checking account with $750. In order for the credit to occur in Tom's checking account, another transaction has to take place first. It is the other side of the transaction which is called a **debit**. Once Chris' check has been cleared through the banking system, Chris' checking account is debited with $750. In banking and finance, there are always two sides for each transaction, a plus side (credit) and a minus side (debit). An account can only be credited with $750 if another account (somewhere else) is debited by the same amount.

In addition to completing the deposit slip, you also have to sign on the back of the check you received. This is called endorsing a check.

**How To Endorse A Check**
When you receive a check from someone you have to endorse that check before you can deposit it into your account. When you are ready to endorse the check, turn the check over and sign your name next to the "X" on the line below the phrase: ENDORSE HERE.

Although there are a number of ways to endorse a check, it is best to use the **safe method** which looks like this:

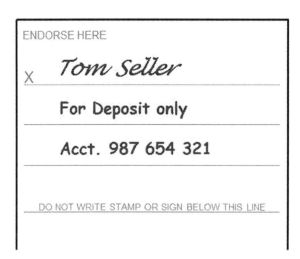

Endorsing the check with this method ensures that it can only be deposited to Tom's account. More specifically, the check can only be credited to an account in Tom's name with the following account number: 987 654 321.

***Think About It:***

*There are other ways to endorse a check. When you just sign the check without specifying "For Deposit only" it means that you give authorization that the check can be cashed by anyone and deposited into any account, not necessarily your own account. If the check gets lost, anyone who finds the check could cash it for himself – that would be like finding money on the street – finders, keepers...*

*Our safe method ensures that the money ends up exactly where you want it. You should use this method of endorsing a check especially if you don't deposit the check directly or in case you ask someone else to deposit the check for you.*

*There is another method of endorsing a check by designating another person to cash the check. The endorsement would specify: "Pay to the order of* <u>John Doe</u>*" and then sign your name just below that. John Doe now becomes the new* **Payee** *and he will have to endorse the check as well before he can deposit the check into his own account. Can you envision some possible problems using this method? Imagine what happens when the person who originally wrote the check doesn't have enough money in his account to pay for the amount? Can you appreciate how messy this could get for all three persons involved in this transaction? Try to think of other potential problems arising from the less safe endorsement methods.*

## Where To Deposit A Check?

There are a number of ways and a number of places to deposit a check. Let's look at the different methods of depositing checks.

<u>Depositing A Check At Your Bank</u>

The best way to deposit a check is the good old way - stepping inside your bank and giving it to the teller along with a completed deposit slip. Although it may be inconvenient to get to your local bank, there are several reasons why I still prefer this method.

- You can get some help in case you have several checks to deposit or in case you have a question.
- A teller double checks your deposit slip and the amounts; the teller can also help spot any errors or problems with a check you may have received. *Remember: Four eyes can see more than two!*

- Lastly, review the receipt from the bank and make sure it matches the totals of all checks you deposited.

The downside is obvious too...

- You can only cash the check during banking hours
- Your nearest bank branch may be far away
- You may have to stand in line and wait a few minutes

By and large, if you want a safe and reliable method of having your checks cashed, visiting your bank may be worth the effort.


Depositing A Check At Your Bank's ATM
ATM's are the next best option to deposit your checks. ATMs give you more convenience because they are accessible 24 hours a day. It is best to use an ATM of your bank. Another bank's ATM may offer the service through a joined network but additional charges may apply and it also takes longer for the amount to appear in your account.

Ideally, you should prepare your deposit slip and endorse the check prior to approaching the ATM. Next, put the deposit slip and check into an ATM deposit envelope (they are usually in holders next to the ATM machine. Then, just follow these steps to deposit your check:

- Insert your debit card into the ATM and enter your PIN number.
- Select Deposits from the on-screen menu.
- Select the account where you want the deposit to go to.
- Enter the amount of your deposit.
- Slip the envelope with your check and deposit slip into the ATM.
- Wait for confirmation that the transaction is complete.
- A receipt for your deposit is printed. Don't forget to take it!

Having said all this, the more advanced ATMs today simply scan your checks and you won't need a deposit slip. But you should still endorse your check with the safe method we just learned. Then follow the same steps as above but instead of slipping it into an envelope, just insert your check into the ATM; the machine will scan everything for you. To be sure everything was scanned correctly, wait for the receipt and check if all the numbers and entries are fine.

### Think About It:
*Making deposits at ATMs can be much more convenient than having to wait inside the bank until a teller is available. Even better, you can make your deposit anytime, day or night whether your bank is open or closed. Can you think of some disadvantages of making ATM deposits? Are they safe? What happens when you make a mistake or another error occurs? If you have many checks to deposit and you want another pair of eyes go over the entries on the deposit slip, it may be worth your while to step inside a bank and have a teller double check everything for you.*

## Depositing A Check At Your Bank's Drop Box

Drop boxes are the just like the drop boxes at libraries – the low-tech versions of today's ATMs. People tend to use drop boxes after banking hours. As with your ATM deposits, prepare your deposit slip and endorse the check(s), place them in the special envelopes provided by the bank. Sadly, the drop boxes don't give you a receipt. Therefore, you should keep a note of the check number, the amount and the name of the person who issued the check just in case the check gets lost. This low-tech option is obviously not the safest method and should only be used for smaller check deposits.

## Depositing A Check Via Remote Deposit

Banks are usually quite open to innovation because innovation and better technology mean lower costs and higher profits. It is therefore no surprise that some banks today offer various forms of new and innovative ways to allow you to hand over your money to them.

The so-called **Remote deposit capture** is a system that can scan checks and transmit the scanned images to your bank for deposit into an account. The system is mostly used by businesses today to allow faster processing of larger numbers of checks. It may not be too long before such a system is available to consumers.

If you are a long-term customer in good standing with your bank, some banks allow you to take photographs of checks and transmit the photos online to your bank. This is mainly for convenience to get the cash to your account faster. However, you still have to mail or drop the checks within a certain period of time. Some banks today offer **iPhone apps** as a fast and convenient way to take a photo of your check and have it transmitted to your account.

**Think About It:**
*These days more and more financial transactions are done without cash. Debit cards, credit cards and electronic transfers have become more popular because they are more convenient than using cash. We previously asked if you can imagine that cash might completely disappear one day; how about checks? Using checks seems more complicated than using credit and debit cards; can you imagine a time when payments by check will disappear? Think of the consequences and consider the pros and cons if checks were to disappear one day.*

☙

## What Not To Do

As we learned, Banks are still the best place to deposit your checks. Yet, people can sometimes be tempted to cash their checks at check cashing shops or payday loan shops since they are often situated near mini malls and convenient central locations. Unless you do not have a bank account, you should never use these places. Their fees for cashing your checks are extremely high. Remember it is your money; don't waste it on some high priced service just because of convenience. We will learn more about the **Do's and Don'ts In Banking** when we wrap up this chapter.

☙

## Balancing Your Check Book

Having learned the basics of checks and check-writing, we now need to figure out how to best manage when numerous checks are written and how to record and keep track of what we spend. More importantly, we want to make sure that no mistakes are made.

Even though checks are only a representation of your money, any mistakes through writing incorrect numbers or not paying attention to detail can end up costing you actual money through fees, penalties or just erroneous transactions. Remember it's your money and you want to be thorough in managing it.

**First Things First: Keeping Track**
Keeping track is essential for anything you do with your money, whether you spend it, save it or invest it.

> ***Think About It:***
> *Why is it so important to keep track of your money?*
>
> *If you don't know how much money you have, where it went and what you spent it on, you are clearly not in control of your finances. Can you think of a situation that is very dangerous, potentially lethal if you are not in control? Imagine driving a car. You have to be in control of the accelerator, brakes and the steering wheel. Not keeping track of where your money is going is a bit like driving a car and letting go of the steering wheel – very dangerous and potentially lethal…*

When it comes to managing your checking account and your check book, the first rule of business is to keep track of everything by writing it down. By the way, the same is true for any other financial transactions including managing your credit cards.

The good news is there are many different ways to keep track of the checks you write and we will cover a few of the most popular methods. It doesn't matter which method you choose, as long as it works for you. However, the key to success in keeping track and managing your money is **consistency**. Choose a method and a system that works for you and that suits your personal preference. Establishing a regular routine and turning it into a habit like brushing your teeth or taking a shower works best and assures the much needed consistency.

**Check Duplicates**
You can track the checks you have been writing by simply using a check book that includes a duplicate (via carbon copy) for each check number. Every time you write a check, the carbon paper copies your hand written entries onto the duplicate check. A small plastic sheet which is part of your check book must be placed between the check you are writing and the unused checks beneath it to prevent the carbon copy from transferring to other duplicates. It takes very little practice to use these types of check books and they are the most convenient way of manually keeping track of your checks. A duplicate check is the thinner paper behind each check and it looks like this:

```
KEEP YOUR DUPLICATE CHECKS IN YOUR CHECKBOOK                                    1001
  ☑ Track your expenses...                    □  TAX DEDUCTIBLE ITEM
  □ Clothing      □ Food         □ Transportation              2 October 2010
  □ Credit Card   □ Utilities    □ Mortgage
  □ Entertainment □ Insurance    □ Other: _____

                                              BALANCE FORWARD
        Tom Seller                            THIS CHECK          750.00
                                              BALANCE
     Seven hundred fifty and 00/100           DEPOSIT
                                              OTHER
                                              NEW BALANCE


        Drums
```

You have to remember to press down firmly on the paper while writing so that all the information is correctly copied onto the duplicate check. After writing the check, tear it off from your check book and you should see the duplicate check. Make sure that all the important information has been copied and is still legible just like the example above.

It is also a good practice to keep all your check books with the duplicate checks for a few years, just in case.

### Check Stubs

Check stubs are included with some check formats. Instead of using a carbon paper to copy the information onto a duplicate check, the stubs remain on the check book but you have to manually enter the payment information of your check a second time.

Perhaps slightly more work you might say but some people prefer using check stubs because it gives them an incentive to go over the payment information twice. It's simply a matter of preference.

Check stubs are still used by traditional accountants who can easily flip through the stubs to find an entry they might be looking for.

Check stubs come in two basic formats. The stubs could be on the left-side of the check or on top of the check.

No matter which format you use, you have to remember to fill in all the information from the check you just wrote. Comparing both entries is a good way to spot mistakes.

In addition to simply entering the details from each check, you should also record the account balances from your checking account. Before Tom wrote the check for his new drum set, he had $1,000 in his checking account. After writing the check, he deducts that amount and is then left with a balance of $250. That information should also go onto the check stub (and the duplicate check if you use the duplicates) to truly keep track of all transactions in your checking account.

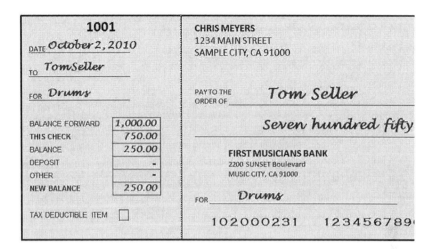

We will discuss more details on this when we learn how to reconcile your checking account.

## Transaction Registers

Transaction Registers are yet another form of keeping track of your checks. Instead of using check stubs or duplicates, the transaction register is usually a separate booklet that fits into your check book. It is essentially a summary table where all your transactions can be listed in an easy to view format. The process of keeping track is basically the same as we learned from the check stubs. You should record the details of each check you wrote in the transaction register.

In addition to recording the transaction details for each check, it is also recommended to compute the balance after each entry. A column with a check mark can be used to indicate which check has been cleared through your bank. (More to come about this when we learn how to reconcile your checking account).

As an example, take a look at how Tom's checking account transactions are recorded in the transaction register. Each deposit is recorded in the Deposit/Credit column and is added to the Balance. Each withdrawal or check payment is entered in the Withdrawal/Balance column and is subtracted from the previous balance. Simple enough isn't it?

| Number or Code | Date | Payee/Transaction Description | □ | Withdrawal, Payment (-) | Deposit, Credit (+) | $ Balance |
|---|---|---|---|---|---|---|
| 1/01/10 | | Account Opening Deposit | | | 500.00 | 500.00 |
| 4/01/10 | DEP | Cash Deposit | | | 250.00 | 750.00 |
| 7/01/10 | DEP | Cash Deposit | | | 250.00 | 1,000.00 |
| 10/02/10 | 1001 | Tom Seller | | 750.00 | | 250.00 |

# Managing Your Checking Account

Taking the tracking process one step further, we can now include any other details of transactions that might occur in your checking account. Sadly, banks sometimes charge fees as we learned in the previous chapters. But some banks also offer interest on certain checking accounts. In order to keep track of everything including fees and interest, the transaction register might be a useful starting point since it allows you to enter any other itemized deposits and withdrawals in addition to the typical check details.

The objective is to match your own records with the bank's records. That matching process is called reconciling or reconciling your check book with the checking account. Here's how this process works:

### Reconciliations
Matching your checking account with your check book is essentially a balancing act with the aim to match the balances of two separate sets of records: Your checking account and your check book. The process is called reconciling or balancing your check book with the checking account. Whichever name you choose, the important part is that you do this task at least once a month, preferably more often especially when you have lots of transactions in your checking account.

෴

# Your First Reconciliation

Things You Need:
- Your most recent bank statement (or online statement)
- Our simple checkbook balancing form (see below)
- Your transaction register or check stubs
- A calculator and pencil

Before you begin, make sure that you have all the necessary information in front of you. The reconciliation then happens in a few steps as follows:

### Step 1
Go through your transaction register or check stub and compare the checks (check # and amounts) with the bank statement. A simple technique is to put a check mark behind each check that is cleared and matches with your check stubs.

If you notice any check payments on the bank statement that do not appear on your check stubs, there might be a problem and you want to mark those payments for more detailed verification later on.

Assuming that all check payments match with the check stubs, we can go on to the next slep. Take the closing balance of your bank statement and write it down. Then add all deposits you may have made to your account that you recorded on your check stubs but aren't showing up on the statement yet.

| | | | | |
|---|---|---|---|---|
| **Closing balance shown on bank statement** | | | a | 255.00 |
| **Add deposits not credited:** | | | | |
| 1 | Check 1 deposited today | | b | 20.00 |
| 2 | Check 2 deposited today | | c | 30.00 |
| 3 | | | d | |
| **Total Deposits not yet credited** | | (b+c+d) | e | 50.00 |
| **Subtotal** | | (a+e) | f | 305.00 |

The bank statement's ending balance is $255. However, your own records show that you made two additional check deposits both of which have not cleared yet and are not on the bank statement. Both amounts have to be added to the bank balance.

Next, you have to subtract any amounts for check payments you made but which are not on the bank statement yet.

**Subtract outstanding checks:**
*checks written but not on bank statement*

| | | | |
|---|---|---|---|
| 1 | Piano Lessons | g | 50.00 |
| 2 | Sheet Music | h | 20.00 |
| 3 | | i | |
| 4 | | j | |
| 5 | | k | |
| **Total outstanding checks** (g+h+i+j+k) | | l | 70.00 |
| **Adjusted Bank Balance** (f minus l) | | | 235.00 |

A total amount of $70 has been paid but has not been cleared through your bank. However, you need to treat this amount as if it has been deducted already even though it doesn't show on the statement yet.

In essence, you added $50 (for the checks you deposited today) to the bank balance and deducted $70 (for the payments you made today) resulting in a net decrease of $20. The adjusted bank balance is therefore $235.

The first major step is complete when the adjusted bank balance equals the amount in your bank account after all these payments and deposits have been cleared. Now you have to make sure that your own transaction register or check stub is adjusted as well.

## Step 2

In your checkbook register, check off each cancelled check returned to you or each check that appears on the check listing, making sure that the amount you recorded is the same amount the bank shows.

You begin by verifying that each deposit on your bank statement is also recorded in your transaction register. Check mark any deposits in your transaction register just like you did for the checks.

| | | | |
|---|---|---|---|
| **Last balance on txn register or check stub** | | a | 230.00 |
| **Add interest or other deposits:** | | | |
| 1 Interest | | b | 15.00 |
| 2 | | c | |
| 3 | | d | |
| **Total Deposits Not Recorded** | (b+c+d) | e | 15.00 |
| **Subtotal** | (a+e) | f | 245.00 |

In our example, an interest payment of $15 has been credited to your account. You could not determine this amount until you saw the statement, but it is a proper deposit in your account and must be included in your transaction register. Your balance is therefore increased by $15, the amount of interest paid to your account.

You then have to examine if there are any withdrawals or payments shown on the bank statement that aren't included in your transaction register yet. Those are usually ATM withdrawals, automatic payments or debit card purchases. But they can also be bank fees or service charges. All of those must be reconciled with your transaction register as well.

| | | | |
|---|---|---|---|
| **Subtract Fees, charges & withdrawals:** | | | |
| *Items not yet recorded on check book* | | | |
| 1 Bank service charge | | g | 10.00 |
| 2 | | h | |
| 3 | | i | |
| 4 | | j | |
| 5 | | k | |
| **Total Fees Not Recorded** | (g+h+i+j+k) | l | 10.00 |
| **Adjusted Check Book Balance** | (f minus l) | | 235.00 |

Your bank charges $10 to give you a number of added services for the checking account. That amount has to be included in your register as well. Deduct the $10 from your balance to end up with a total adjusted check book balance of $235.

Verifying the bank records and your own personal records side by side is the ideal way to reconcile your check book with the checking account. When all transactions are included on both records, the balances should match.

Here is a summary again of both sides of the reconciliation process:

| Bank Statement | | Check Book | |
|---|---|---|---|
| Closing balance shown on bank statement | a 255.00 | Last balance on txn register or check stub | a 230.00 |
| **Add deposits not credited:** | | **Add interest or other deposits:** | |
| 1  Check 1 deposited today | b 20.00 | 1  Interest | b 15.00 |
| 2  Check 2 deposited today | c 30.00 | 2 | c |
| 3 | d | 3 | d |
| Total Deposits not yet credited (b+c+d) | e 50.00 | Total Deposits Not Recorded (b+c+d) | e 15.00 |
| Subtotal (a+e) | f 305.00 | Subtotal (a+e) | f 245.00 |
| **Subtract outstanding checks:** *checks written but not on bank statement* | | **Subtract Fees, charges & withdrawals:** *Items not yet recorded on check book* | |
| 1  Piano Lessons | g 50.00 | 1  Bank service charge | g 10.00 |
| 2  Sheet Music | h 20.00 | 2 | h |
| 3 | i | 3 | i |
| 4 | j | 4 | j |
| 5 | k | 5 | k |
| Total outstanding checks (g+h+i+j+k) | l 70.00 | Total Fees Not Recorded (g+h+i+j+k) | l 10.00 |
| Adjusted Bank Balance (f minus l) | 235.00 | Adjusted Check Book Balance (f minus l) | 235.00 |

You can download a blank reconciliation worksheet from resource page (see resource section of this book).

### An Old Accounting Trick

*In our example, the reconciliation worked perfectly and in most cases, you should easily reconcile your accounts within a few minutes. Sometimes however, your balances can be off by a few cents and you cannot seem to find the error(s). Use an old accounting trick in this case: If the difference between the two records divides evenly by nine, you may have just messed up the order of one of your numbers a.k.a a transposed number. This is one of the most common mistakes in data entry and with this simple trick you can easily spot it.*

*Examples:*
*If you wrote in your register $25.59 instead of $25.95 – the difference is 36 cents which divides into 9 four times even. Or enter $10.36 instead of $10.63 – the difference is 27 cents which divides into 9 three times even.*

## Why Reconcile?
The main rationale for verifying all transactions in your bank accounts is centered in the principle of being in control of your finances. That means you need to be aware of your actual account balance all the time. Banks can make mistakes and they tend NOT to be in your favor. Therefore it is always a good idea to review your statements carefully.

Another important rationale for reconciliations arises from a time lag that exists between the day you write the check and the day that the funds are actually deducted from your checking account.

This process usually takes a couple of days but it can sometimes take a week or longer. Don't forget that the people you are paying may not deposit your check for a while. Therefore, you should be aware of the actual balance in your bank account inclusive of all the checks you have been writing even if they don't show up on your bank statement. Your checks will eventually be cashed and you must have enough money in your account to cover the checks you write. If you don't have enough money in your checking account, the check will bounce i.e. it will be returned to the bank your payee deposited it.

## Reconciliations with Accounting Software
Today, there are numerous software applications that can help you keep track of your money and your bank transactions. Some of them have built-in reconciliation functions. Others make the reconciling of checks and payments very easy. No matter what system you use, you should still be aware of the basic principles of keeping track and reconciling your accounts. And, you have to be consistent and update your system just like you would have to update your transaction register. We cover some additional tips on systems and software in an upcoming chapter.

## What Happens When You Bounce a Check?
Bouncing a check is not to be taken lightly. Banks usually charge steep fees for bounced checks and it is rather embarrassing having to explain yourself to the person you paid why the check was returned.

If you bounce checks a few times, it may also adversely affect your credit history. As you would have guessed, certain vendors may stop accepting checks from you altogether.

Long story short, you want to make sure you remember who you paid and how much you paid. You should know exactly how much your effective checking account balance is before you pay someone with a check. Reconciling your checking account is therefore an important task that should be done regularly and thoroughly.

***Think About It:***

*Say you bought a few CDs at a record store and paid for them with a check, $50 in total. You have a rough idea of the balance in your checking account which should be about $100 right now. However, you forgot that the renewal of your annual subscription to Napster is automatically deducted from your checking account today as well. The actual balance in your bank account was only $98 and with the $50 subscription deducted for Napster, the account has only $48 left.*

*The record store deposits your check with its bank the same day and that bank needs to clear your check with your bank. But when your check is presented it has insufficient funds for payment and is returned to the record store's bank. You end up paying a bounced check fee of $25 charged by your bank. Worse yet, you're on the hook for another $27 (charged by the record store's bank to the record store) which you have to end up paying as well if you want to stay on good terms with the record store and avoid any type of legal issues.*

*All in all, a simple oversight can cost you dearly. In this case, your $50 worth of records eventually cost you $102 ($50 + $25 + $27). In addition to the painful charges, it is also a big hassle and it's embarrassing. Store owners have a near photographic memory for people who bounce checks – don't do it too often! Lesson learned: It pays to remember the balance in your account <u>before</u> writing a check.*

༈

## 5 Easy Ways To Bounce A Check – Don't Do These...

- You simply forget to balance your checkbook
- You forget to enter a check payment, debit card purchase, or automatic payment in your transaction register; you overestimate how much money you have in your account.
- You write a check knowing you don't have enough money to cover the check but you expect to receive a big enough deposit before the check clears.
- You write a check knowing you don't have enough money to cover the check but you hope to make a deposit in cash before the check you wrote clears.

- You receive a check from someone and that check bounces. If you counted on the funds from this check before it actually cleared and wrote one or more checks to pay for things, some of those checks may bounce as well. In addition, you have to pay painful fees.

## A Warning On Bouncing Checks

Bouncing a check should really not be taken lightly at all. In fact, in some cases it could lead to criminal charges if there is intent to defraud involved. Since most people cover their bad checks reasonably soon, criminal charges happen rarely. However, if a check was written with no intent or no means to actually pay the stated amount, the writer of the check could be in trouble. Each state has its own set of laws governing checks and you would be well advised to read up on the basic legal requirements in your state.

Bouncing a check does not usually show up on your credit report. However, if your bounced check is for a large amount and the company you wanted to pay turns over your bounced check to a collection agency, it will impact your credit report. It could also happen that the company reports your bounced check as a late payment which can show up on your credit report.

### Think About It:
*Having learned all this, you may think twice before writing a check from now on. The downside of writing bad checks in other countries is much worse. In certain countries, you'll end up in jail immediately and you will stay there until the amount is paid in full including fees and penalties.*

## Overdraft Protection

As we just learned, bouncing a check can result in painful fees which are completely unnecessary.

Most banks offer a service called overdraft protection which can help prevent overdrafts and bounced checks. Usually, you will need a savings account which is linked to your checking account. If a transaction exceeds the balance in your checking account, additional funds from your linked savings account will be transferred to your checking account automatically.

There are some caveats though. Banks usually charge a monthly fee for this service. In addition, they require you to maintain a minimum balance in your checking or savings account. If balances fall below those limits, additional fees may be charged again.

Please also be aware that writing a check that exceeds the combined balances in both accounts will still bounce.

In summary, it still pays to be fully aware of all transactions in your account(s) and to reconcile your bank account(s) often. The more transactions you have the more often you should reconcile.

∽

## Tips For Online Banking

A growing number of banking services and financial transactions have been conducted over the Internet. Increasingly, financial institutions are looking to conduct most of their business online. There are some banks with no retail branches at all, conducting all their business exclusively online or via telephone.

Whether you use online banking, telephone banking or an ATM, security is of utmost importance. You should apply the basic safeguards and common sense to all your transactions. Security is equally important for the protection of your data as well as the bank's data. Therefore, most banks have very sophisticated security procedures in place. A good bank should have guarantees for your online privacy and provide indemnities against breach of online security.

> ### *Think About It:*
> *Apply the following logic to your security concerns about online banking: If a bank didn't provide the most advanced security features and security breaches were to occur, the bank would have a hard time keeping their customers. The slightest notion of a bank not being able to manage online security would have most customers running for the doors. As long as you deal with a reputable bank that has branches nationwide and is insured by the Federal Deposit Insurance Corporation (FDIC), you can be reasonably certain that their online banking security is up to par. However, it never hurts to be vigilant. Check the transactions in your online account frequently and reconcile all your accounts on a regular basis; it will minimize potential damage. If anything does not look right, call up your bank and find out. If you are not sure whether your bank is FDIC insured, you can find out directly from the FDIC on this site:*
>
> *http://www2.fdic.gov/idasp/main_bankfind.asp*

If you suspect any fraud on your account, immediate action is paramount. The same is true for identity theft; the faster you act the better. Immediately call your bank and ask them to temporarily suspend your online banking access. Your bank will also provide you with some other useful tips and help you to re-establish security. We will provide more information about general security measures and dealing with identity theft when we cover credit and credit cards.

### A Word On Spam And Phishing Emails

As technology advances, the crooks are also learning new tricks. If you use email, you must have come across emails that look as if they come from your bank but are in fact from crooks trying to gain access to your online passwords or account details. Those emails are called phishing emails and they are much worse than regular spam or junk mail. Some of these phishing emails ask you to update your password; others will tempt you into revealing your personal details by suggesting that your account may be suspended if you don't update your personal information.

No matter how authentic that email might look like, rest assured that no bank will send you an email asking you to update your password. Whatever the message might say, DO NOT CLICK ON THE LINKS THEY PROVIDE. Instead, call up your bank and verify whether anything needs to be updated or if any account or account activity may have been suspended. You can also check your account online, but please do so by directly opening your browser and going to your normal bank account online access. As a general rule, if you don't know the person or originator of the email, simply delete it.

ᏬᎧ

## Basic Online Security Tips

- You should never give out any of your account information, username or password to anyone – especially NOT via email.
- Avoid simple passwords with your initials and birthdates. Instead, create passwords that are difficult for others to guess.
- Change your passwords often!
- Always use a combination of letters and numbers.
- Avoid online banking transactions on shared computers (Internet Cafés, libraries or other public online access networks). If you have to use a shared computer, make sure to always log off and close the browser once you're finished with online banking.
- Verify that your bank's web address begins with https://
- You should also see a lock icon on the bottom of your browser.

- Do not click on links embedded in suspicious emails.
- If you notice unusual transactions or money missing from your account, notify your bank immediately.

ᔐ

## Making Sure The Banks Treat You Right

**Don't forget: It's your money!**
Do you like gadgets? Getting your hands on the latest mobile phone, iPod or computer game is certainly tempting. The temptation is even higher when retailers offer additional freebies that come along with the latest gadget. Mobile phones are often given away for free if you sign up with a particular mobile phone carrier for, say, a minimum 2-year contract.

This may come as a surprise, but banks have been giving out these kinds of freebies for a long time. They know very well what it takes to get a new client and they have long been using gifts and other incentives to entice you to open an account with them.

Years ago particularly in England, they used toasters and tea kettles. Other banks gave away magazine subscriptions, movie and theatre tickets, coolers, camping gear, calculators etc. Banks have been giving away free toys and stuffed animals to get younger kids to part with their piggy banks and open a savings account.

The incentives are always better when you put more money on the table. Open an account with, say, $3,000 or more and a bank might give you a free MP3 player. You might get a digital camera if you open an account with $2,000 and agree to keep your account for a year or pay your bills via the Internet.

> **Think About It:**
> When we talked about interest, we learned that your interest rate is usually higher when you commit your CD or fixed deposit account for a longer period of time. We also found out that the interest rate is slightly better for larger deposits. The same concept applies when you open an account. The larger your account opening deposit, the bigger and flashier are the freebies. Can you think of other incentives a bank may give?

When you consider opening a bank account, you should look beyond the free gifts and never let those "gifts" cloud your judgment. More important than flashy toys are the services the bank provides and the terms offered, as well as any fees and charges for your account. You should take your time in selecting the right bank as well as the right types of accounts. My general rule of thumb is that basic checking and savings accounts should always be free of service charges.

Remember, **it's your money** that's sitting in the bank! You are just letting the bank keep it for a while. For the privilege of using your money, they owe you something in return. You should never have to pay for having someone use your money!

### Reality Check:

*If I had to choose between a digital camera and completely free checking accounts and free transactions, the choice would be easy for me. I would forget about the digital camera and be more interested in what the bank can offer me in terms of free services that work best for me.*

*Finding the right bank with the right combination of accounts and additional services can be confusing. However, if you are opening your first bank account, chances are that a combination of free checking and savings account would be more than adequate to get you started. When the time comes and you have more experience with your bank and know more about banking and investing, you can always convert your accounts then. In the beginning, the basic banking services should be free of charge. No matter how flashy the free gift is that your friendly banker waves in front of you, remember that you might have to pay for it in some other way that could cost you more in the long run. There are plenty of banks out there to choose from, if the bank wants your business they should give you something in return. However, more important than all other bells and whistles are safety, reliability and the level and quality of their services.*

### More On Bank Fees And Service Charges

Most people use a checking account to pay some bills and increasingly pay for the majority of their expenses with debit and credit cards. When you have a basic free checking account, the bank might limit the number of checks you can write each month. They might also ask you to maintain a minimum balance in the checking account and charge a so-called "maintenance fee" each month if your balance falls below a certain minimum, say $500. Some banks are a bit sneaky and calculate a daily average balance that needs to be maintained to avoid any fees. Be careful and always check your bank statement, preferably a few times each month. This is not only good for security, in case of fraud, but also to spot any errors or fees that you may not have been aware of. Remember, it's your money; you should always keep an eye on it!

### Think About It:

In general, banks are quite creative when it comes to finding new ways to charge fees. Charging you a fee if your "average daily balance" is below a certain amount is a bit sneaky because you don't know exactly how much that average is until the end of the month. To be on the safe side, you might keep too much of your money in the checking account where it earns no interest. Ideally, you should only keep a relatively small amount in your checking account, just enough to cover your usual monthly expenses. Any additional money should be in a savings account where it could earn some interest.

Most banks are somewhat flexible when it comes to the services and terms on offer. Remember they compete for your money! As we learned before, the more money you have to open an account, the happier your banker will be. If you have a lot of money already, you will find that some bankers bend over backwards to get you as a client. By contrast, they are not so flexible if you only have say $100 to open an account. In that case, it might be more difficult to negotiate something other than their standard rates.

As you start out with banking, you may have to do a lot more things on your own to avoid charges. However, the good news is that this is actually the best way to learn about banking. You might make some mistakes along the way but if you pay attention, you can learn how to tweak the bank's services so that it works just right for you.

As you get better at banking and once you have a little more money on deposit with the bank, you can suggest to your bank that they should consider your combined account balance and no longer assess any extra fees for more transactions, or any fees for checks. In return, you could promise them to do all your banking with them. They are always happy to hear that!

# Do's and Don'ts Of Banking

Choosing a bank that's exactly right for you is no easy feat. There are hundreds of retail banks around. Most of them offer very similar services and terms. You might ask your friends or family for a recommendation and in the end you can narrow your choices to a handful of banks.

The large nation-wide financial behemoths offer the widest range of services but they are also the most profit-driven of the lot. Do not mistake their friendly advertising slogans for sincere caring about your financial well-being. The banks care about their own profits first and foremost, something which we all learned only too well during and after the global financial crisis of 2008/2009.

My sentiment towards banks has always been a love/hate relationship. **You can't live with them but you cannot live without them either.** Know that they are in the business of making money from your money and that's that. Keep that in mind when negotiating any type of deal with your bank.

Once again, never ever forget that the bank has <u>your</u> money for safe keeping. There are hundreds of other banks who can do the same safe-keeping job just as well. If there is anything you don't like about your bank or its service, tell your bank how you feel about it. If they cannot accommodate you, the door is always open. Take your money elsewhere and find a bank that works better for you.

Community Banks and Credit Unions are slightly higher in my ranking but be aware that they sometimes cannot offer the same breadth of services as the larger nation-wide banks. Of the two, the Credit Unions deserve a second look.

Credit unions are mutual companies or cooperatives that are owned and controlled by its members i.e. the people who have an account with them. Their main purpose is often to promote sustainable local community development and to provide credit at reasonable rates. They still offer most of the traditional banking services but are typically more customer-focused because of the simple fact that the customers are also their shareholders. Credit Unions in the US are "Not-For-Profit Organizations".

In choosing a bank or credit union, you should do some comparison shopping just like you would with any major financial transaction. The best way to find out if a bank works for you is to try out a few of them. It may be a little more work in terms of keeping track of your finances, but it certainly won't hurt to open several accounts with different banks or credit unions to see if their services work for you. That also makes things a lot easier if you're not happy with one of the banks. Simply say goodbye and transfer your money to the other bank. When the time comes and you have accumulated more wealth, it also makes sense to open accounts with several banks. The FDIC provides a deposit guarantee which is currently at $250,000 per account. If you have accumulated more savings and financial assets, diversify and spread your assets across several banks. As we will learn later on diversification is an important concept in financial risk management. Spreading your deposits across more than one bank is also a form of diversification.

## Places To Avoid

You may or may not agree with me in the way I approach my ongoing love-hate relationship towards banks. Suffice it to say that they provide an important service to our economy. Individuals and companies simply would not be able to function as efficiently in today's modern society without the basic banking and financial services these institutions provide. In terms of banking services, you're best served dealing with credit unions and banks.

However, there are some places you should clearly avoid at all cost.

People can sometimes be tempted to cash their checks at check cashing shops since they are often situated near mini malls and convenient central locations. Unless you do not have a bank account, you should never use these places. Their fees for cashing your checks are extremely high.

Payday loan shops are to be avoided as well. They are essentially credit sharks that lurk around in mini malls and increasingly online. Their interest rates and fees are atrocious. Do not use them!

Unless your life depends on it, find another way to finance your cash needs. Remember it is your money. Don't waste it on some high priced service just because of convenience!

# FOUR

## *Credit, Credit Cards & Loans*

Consumer credit, credit cards and various ways of financing have become an essential part of today's economy. No industry has been untouched by the pervasive use of credit. Consumers keep buying things they cannot afford but feel they need to have them right away. Many consumers feel they are better off paying for things later so they can own those things today.

Without a doubt, the global economy would come to a standstill if credit were to dry up completely. During the financial crisis of 2008/2009 we saw a glimpse of what could happen when the well of instant credit dries up. No one can deny that the global economy, in particular the U.S., needs a functioning system for financing and credit. However, we have to understand the implications of incurring too much debt. Two important factors are interest rates and the time value of money, both of which we just looked at. As we will learn in the following pages, the impact of too much credit on your personal finances can be devastating. We will get you in the right mood by showing some of the scary sides of credit cards first. You will also learn how important it is to understand credit and to use your credit wisely.

### Statistics on Plastics

Before we learn what credit is all about, let's look at some insightful statistics. The following numbers will give you an idea as to how widespread credit cards are in our society.

- In 2010, the average credit card debt per U.S. household (that had credit card debt) was $15,788. The total of all credit cards in circulation in the U.S. was 576.4 million, as of year-end 2009[18].
- On average, U.S. card holders have 3.5 credit cards[19].
- Average interest rate (APR) on new credit card offers: 14.10%[20].
- Average interest rate (APR) on existing credit cards is 14.67%[21].
- 4.27% of US credit cards have late payments of 60 days or longer[22].
- 13.01% of US credit cards are not being paid back and default[23].

18 Nilson Report, February 2010
19 The Survey of Consumer Payment Choice, Federal Reserve Boston, Jan-2010
20 CreditCards.com Weekly Rate Report, May 2010
21 Federal Reserve's G.19 report on consumer credit, May 2010
22 Fitch Ratings, April 2010
23 Fitch Ratings, April 2010

- U.S. consumer debt (excl. mortgages): $2.46 trillion[24].
- Total U.S. consumer debt (including mortgages): $11.7 trillion[25].

༄

## What Is Credit?

Credit comes from the Latin word "credere" which means to trust or to believe. Lending money to someone involves a good amount of trust, namely the person using the credit will pay back the amount that is owed. Credit can be given in various forms. It is essentially the amount of money that you can borrow at any given time.  For example, this could be in form of a credit line with your bank. The most popular type of credit though comes in the form of credit cards. Exactly how much credit is given to you shows up in the credit limit on your credit card. In simple terms, the more credit worthy you are, the more money you are able to borrow.

Until you use credit, you don't actually owe anything. Just think of it as a financial resource that you can tap into if needed. Once credit is taken, for instance by purchasing a new microphone with your credit card, some of your credit then turns into debt which needs to be paid back within the terms of the credit card agreement. It all sounds a lot more complicated than it is.  Let's do an example to clarify these terms.

Meet Erica, the singer. She needs a new microphone for an important performance. Her credit card has a credit limit of $5,000. A new microphone costs $250 and Erica feels she can use her credit to pay for this purchase.

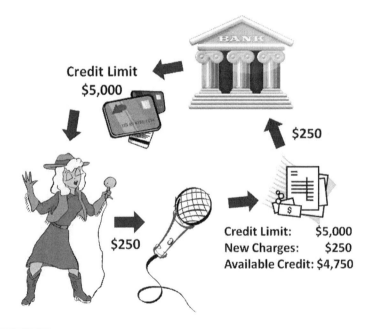

Credit Limit
$5,000

$250

$250

Credit Limit:        $5,000
New Charges:       $250
Available Credit: $4,750

---

24 Federal Reserve's G.19 report on consumer credit, May 2010
25 Federal Reserve Bank of New York, Consumer Credit Panel, 2010

When her credit card statement arrives, the charge for the new micro-phone is listed. Her existing credit limit is now reduced by $250 giving her a remaining credit limit of $4,750. Once Erica pays back the full amount, her credit limit goes back to $5,000.

You can see that Erica could (in theory) tap into her entire credit limit which is called "maxing out" the credit card. I strongly recommend AGAINST doing that. Erica is best advised to pay her charges in full to avoid high interest payments. We will soon learn why.

∽

## What You Need To Know About Credit Cards

Despite some of the many negative aspects of credit cards, they do pro-vide an important service for the functioning of modern commerce. Internet companies like eBay or Amazon simply would not exist today if it wasn't for the widespread use of "plastic" money. To take advantage of the positive aspects of credit cards it is important to understand the pros and cons first.

### Positive Aspects
Say you just received a new credit card with a $5,000 credit limit. The credit card company is therefore giving you free range to spend up to $5,000 as you please. So knock yourself out! But wait!  Is there a catch?

Well of course there is. This credit comes with terms & conditions attached – lots of them to be sure. Tempting as it may be, it's best if you don't use up all of your $5,000 credit. You should only consider maxing out your credit card if you already have the cash to pay the full amount when the balance is due.

Take the example of Erica again. She used $250 of her $5,000 credit limit to buy a new microphone. When the credit card statement arrives, she is given a time limit of a couple of weeks to pay for the $250 balance.

Two important aspects of money show up when credit is taken and is turned into debt:  Time and the interest rate that kicks in when the bal-ance is not paid in full.

Since Erica is still young and doesn't have a long credit history, the interest rate on her credit card is 29.99%. At that rate, it makes a lot more sense for her to pay the full amount back to the credit card company right away. When Erica pays the balance before the due date the credit limit on her card goes back to $5,000.

### What About Those Positive Aspects Then?
a) Using a credit card to pay for a purchase is simply convenient.  Plastic fits into almost any size pocket or purse. It is easier and safer than carrying

cash around. Swiping a card is also more convenient than having to fill out a check and tracking the check in your transaction register. So convenience is a big plus.

b) Erica has a credit limit of $5,000. In essence she is given free money to use for a few weeks from the time of purchase until she actually has to pay for it. That is a big advantage and in theory, Erica could have used up the entire $5,000 until the payment due date.

c) Many credit cards offer additional incentives enticing you to use your card as often as possible. For instance, some cards offer certain cash rewards or points. Other cards give you frequent-flyer miles, typically one mile for each dollar you spend (some special programs even offer double miles).

These are all definite benefits that you can take advantage of. If you are disciplined enough and don't abuse your credit, the convenience, the incentives and the ability to use free cash for a limited period of time are the great benefits of credit cards. There is of course plenty of reason to be cautious – extremely cautious, that is.

### Be Careful With Your Credit

Using "free money", albeit for a short while only, is very tempting. If, and only if, you are disciplined and financially able to pay the full balance back should you ever consider getting close to using your entire credit line. If you can afford your purchase and you have the cash anyway, you might as well use the convenience of credit giving you a few more weeks before actually paying for your purchase.

Perhaps equally important is this underlying temptation to spend money. In fact, that's exactly what your credit card company is banking on: The temptation to use the money just because it's there. It's the same temptation that entices you to buy something you probably won't need, but because it's on sale, creates a false sense of "must have it."

Plastic or electronic money is money nevertheless. Realize that you must fight this deceiving feeling which seemingly makes it easier to part with your money. Every cent you spend with your credit card is a cent spent by you! The consequence shows up as early as your next credit card statement. Be extremely careful not to spend more than you can afford!

We are now going to learn what happens when you don't pay your full credit card balance. We will also look at some of the consequence of late payments. Buckle up. This is when it gets interesting!

### Negative Aspects of Credit Cards

To truly understand the downside of credit cards, we have to revisit the basics of compound interest and the time value of money. Since essentially all credit cards charge double-digit interest, we can already anticipate that any outstanding balance which is not paid in full can easily grow into much larger debt rather quickly.

The easiest way to get a sense of what's at stake comes courtesy of the good old **Rule of 72** which we covered in chapter 2. Here's a quick reminder of how the rule of 72 worked:

The Rule of 72 is a simplified way to determine how long an investment will take to double, given a fixed compound interest rate.

---

**72 ÷ interest rate =  # of years it takes to double your money**

---

Now let's assume that <u>YOU</u> are the credit card company and your investment is the loan you gave to Erica. Erica has two things going against her in terms of credit risk: a) she is young with very little credit history and b) she is a musician which is often associated with someone who doesn't have a regular job and may have a harder time paying bills. Because of these two factors, Erica's interest rate on credit card balances is a whopping 29.99% which is essentially 30%.

You can now easily calculate how this investment performs if Erica does not pay her balance in full at the end of the month.

$$72 ÷ 30 \ (\%) = 2.4 \ (years)$$

If Erica wasn't going to pay her balance back, compound interest would accrue at a rate of 30% per year. In this case, the credit card company could double its investment every 2.4 years. What a great investment for the credit card company and a lousy deal for Erica.

From Erica's perspective, this type of deal could be devastating if she isn't careful. We are now ready to take a closer look at some examples to see how an unpaid balance can easily spiral into a much larger debt.

### Erica's Payment Choices
The best option for Erica is to pay off her credit card balance in full when it's due. Here are some other payment options for Erica. See for yourself what the pros and cons of these payment options are.

### Scenario A
Suppose Erica pays $25 each month on her credit card balance. At 29.99%, it would take her one year to pay off the balance. The table below shows her payment schedule. See how it takes her an entire year to gradually pay off the balance.

| Month | Beginning Balance | Interest | Payment | Principle Paid | Ending Balance |
|---|---|---|---|---|---|
| 1 | $250.00 | $6.25 | $25.00 | $18.75 | $231.25 |
| 2 | $231.25 | $5.78 | $25.00 | $19.22 | $212.03 |
| 3 | $212.03 | $5.30 | $25.00 | $19.70 | $192.33 |
| 4 | $192.33 | $4.81 | $25.00 | $20.19 | $172.13 |
| 5 | $172.13 | $4.30 | $25.00 | $20.70 | $151.43 |
| 6 | $151.43 | $3.78 | $25.00 | $21.22 | $130.22 |
| 7 | $130.22 | $3.25 | $25.00 | $21.75 | $108.47 |
| 8 | $108.47 | $2.71 | $25.00 | $22.29 | $86.18 |
| 9 | $86.18 | $2.15 | $25.00 | $22.85 | $63.34 |
| 10 | $63.34 | $1.58 | $25.00 | $23.42 | $39.92 |
| 11 | $39.92 | $1.00 | $25.00 | $24.00 | $15.92 |
| 12 | $15.92 | $0.40 | $16.32 | $15.92 | $0.00 |

In total, Erica would have paid $41.32 in interest. The actual price for her microphone then would go up to $291.32 ($250 + $41.32).

## Scenario B

Suppose now that Erica pays only $10 each month. It would now take her about 40 months (over three years) to pay off her credit card debt and she would have paid over $147 in interest. Her microphone would cost $397.

| Month | Beginning Balance | Interest | Payment | Principle Paid | Ending Balance |
|---|---|---|---|---|---|
| 1 | $250.00 | $6.25 | $10.00 | $3.75 | $246.25 |
| 2 | $246.25 | $6.15 | $10.00 | $3.85 | $242.40 |
| 3 | $242.40 | $6.06 | $10.00 | $3.94 | $238.46 |
| 4 | $238.46 | $5.96 | $10.00 | $4.04 | $234.42 |
| 5 | $234.42 | $5.86 | $10.00 | $4.14 | $230.28 |
| 6 | $230.28 | $5.76 | $10.00 | $4.24 | $226.03 |
| 7 | $226.03 | $5.65 | $10.00 | $4.35 | $221.68 |
| 8 | $221.68 | $5.54 | $10.00 | $4.46 | $217.22 |
| 9 | $217.22 | $5.43 | $10.00 | $4.57 | $212.65 |
| 10 | $212.65 | $5.31 | $10.00 | $4.69 | $207.97 |
| 11 | $207.97 | $5.20 | $10.00 | $4.80 | $203.16 |
| 12 | $203.16 | $5.08 | $10.00 | $4.92 | $198.24 |
| 13 | $198.24 | $4.95 | $10.00 | $5.05 | $193.19 |
| 14 | $193.19 | $4.83 | $10.00 | $5.17 | $188.02 |
| 15 | $188.02 | $4.70 | $10.00 | $5.30 | $182.72 |
| 16 | $182.72 | $4.57 | $10.00 | $5.43 | $177.29 |
| 17 | $177.29 | $4.43 | $10.00 | $5.57 | $171.72 |
| 18 | $171.72 | $4.29 | $10.00 | $5.71 | $166.01 |
| 19 | $166.01 | $4.15 | $10.00 | $5.85 | $160.16 |
| 20 | $160.16 | $4.00 | $10.00 | $6.00 | $154.16 |
| 21 | $154.16 | $3.85 | $10.00 | $6.15 | $148.02 |
| 22 | $148.02 | $3.70 | $10.00 | $6.30 | $141.71 |
| 23 | $141.71 | $3.54 | $10.00 | $6.46 | $135.26 |
| 24 | $135.26 | $3.38 | $10.00 | $6.62 | $128.64 |
| 25 | $128.64 | $3.21 | $10.00 | $6.79 | $121.85 |
| 26 | $121.85 | $3.05 | $10.00 | $6.95 | $114.90 |
| 27 | $114.90 | $2.87 | $10.00 | $7.13 | $107.77 |
| 28 | $107.77 | $2.69 | $10.00 | $7.31 | $100.46 |
| 29 | $100.46 | $2.51 | $10.00 | $7.49 | $92.97 |
| 30 | $92.97 | $2.32 | $10.00 | $7.68 | $85.30 |
| 31 | $85.30 | $2.13 | $10.00 | $7.87 | $77.43 |
| 32 | $77.43 | $1.94 | $10.00 | $8.06 | $69.36 |
| 33 | $69.36 | $1.73 | $10.00 | $8.27 | $61.10 |
| 34 | $61.10 | $1.53 | $10.00 | $8.47 | $52.62 |
| 35 | $52.62 | $1.32 | $10.00 | $8.68 | $43.94 |
| 36 | $43.94 | $1.10 | $10.00 | $8.90 | $35.04 |
| 37 | $35.04 | $0.88 | $10.00 | $9.12 | $25.91 |
| 38 | $25.91 | $0.65 | $10.00 | $9.35 | $16.56 |
| 39 | $16.56 | $0.41 | $10.00 | $9.59 | $6.97 |
| 40 | $6.97 | $0.17 | $7.15 | $6.98 | $0 |

Scenario C

The last scenario involves paying only the minimum payment amount let's assume it is $7.50 each month. A detailed payment schedule would be too long to show on these pages. But if you do the math, you can see that Erica would need about 6 years to pay off her balance. She would also pay a total of $293.92 in interest **which is more than the microphone originally cost.** The final price for her microphone would then be **$543.92.** Was it worth that much?

The Federal Reserve Website has a free credit card payment calculator that tells how long it would take to pay off your credit card balance at a given monthly payment:

www.federalreserve.gov/creditcardcalculator

Alternatively, you can download various credit card payment calculators from our resource site (see resource section of this book).

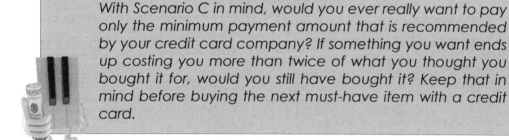

> **_Think About It:_**
> With Scenario C in mind, would you ever really want to pay only the minimum payment amount that is recommended by your credit card company? If something you want ends up costing you more than twice of what you thought you bought it for, would you still have bought it? Keep that in mind before buying the next must-have item with a credit card.

## Time Value of Money & Credit Cards

You may recall the impact of compound interest over time. Compound interest is an exponential function and the dangers of exponential growth are often underestimated. While the time value of money works in your favor when saving and investing, it works very much against you when you owe money and have to pay interest on your debt.

Let us examine an extreme case of exponential growth with a longer time horizon. A typical credit card interest rate for people with less than perfect credit scores is 29.99% as in Erica's case. Let's assess the impact of such an interest rate over a 15 year time period. Let's also assume that YOU are the credit card company earning the 29.99% annual interest from Erica. If you could make that kind of return on say $1,000 compounded at 29.99%, the investment would grow to $17,906 within 10 years. Better yet, it would end up at $66,460 in 15 years.

If you still wonder why credit card companies give you all these incentives to spend more money, here's why: The rates they charge you provide an incredible return for them, a return unmatched by any other type of investment in stocks, bonds or other asset classes.

The graph below speaks for itself.

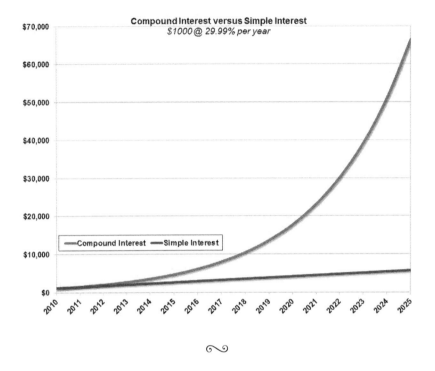

Compound Interest versus Simple Interest
$1000 @ 29.99% per year

❧

## Convenience Checks

Every once in a while you may receive a bunch of checks along with your credit card statement. A free gift from your card issuer perhaps?

The so-called convenience checks look tempting indeed. Convenience checks are just a misleading advertising gimmick. They should really be considered as yet another ingenious way the card issuers are trying to entice you to spend money you don't have so they can earn a ton of interest from you. Here's how convenience checks work:

When credit card companies send you convenience checks, they usually send you a set of four checks. Each of those checks can be used just like any other check and you can pay any of your typical purchases by just filling out the name of the payee and the amount.

You could also make the check out to yourself and deposit it into your own checking account (bad idea by the way).

Some people might argue that these checks are indeed a convenient way to pay for some of your purchases. Whatever their argument may be, the only thing you should ever do with these checks is to **shred them** the minute you receive them. Here's why:

Some card issuers offer their new clients introductory convenience checks at 0% interest for a limited time only. They also show up as special offers on balance transfers (if you transfer your existing balance from another credit card company). However, none of these checks come completely free. You will be charged either percentage of the check amount, usually 3%, or a minimum fee of $5 or more.

The real killer though, for any normal convenience check or whenever the time limit has expired, the charges on these checks are massive. The interest rate on convenience checks is much higher than your normal APR (Annual Percentage Rate) on credit card purchases. If your normal APR was 15%, the APR on convenience checks would typically be closer to 30%. Yes, the card issuer assumes an interest rate that puts you in the same category as some of the least credit worthy customers! It gets worse...

Unlike normal credit card purchases, the interest starts the day you cash the check. Your statement may arrive three weeks after you cashed your convenience check and even if you were to pay your card balance in full, interest would have accumulated between the day of cashing the check and the day you pay off the card balance. In essence, the credit card firms treat convenience checks just like cash advances and balance transfers. All of these methods are great money makers for the card issuers mainly due to the huge interest charged, no matter how high your credit score may be.

In terms of security, convenience checks pose another problem. They require no signature verification and can easily be stolen, leaving you with the hassle of proving that fraud was involved. Unless you can prove that someone stole your convenience checks, you will be liable for the full amount.

To sum it all up, convenience checks should simply be banned. In the meantime, the best course of action is to **shred every single convenience check the minute you receive them.**

If you still don't believe me, let's look at an example:

Take Erica as an example one more time. Say Erica received 4 convenience checks from her card issuer. She was planning to buy a new microphone anyway, so these checks actually come in handy. The new microphone costs $250 and she can just write out a check to the music store for $250 to get her new mike. So now she's thinking, "there are three more checks here. Why not use them up and cash another $250 for each check?" In total, Erica cashes $750 for deposit into her savings account.

After a month, she receives her card statement and is shocked to see all those additional charges she hadn't expected.

෧෨

## Erica's Credit Card Statement

| Checks | Amount | Fees @ 3% | Interest 28 days | Total Charges |
|---|---|---|---|---|
| Convenience Check #1 | $250.00 | $7.50 | $5.75 | $13.25 |
| Convenience Check #2 | $250.00 | $7.50 | $5.75 | $13.25 |
| Convenience Check #3 | $250.00 | $7.50 | $5.75 | $13.25 |
| Convenience Check #4 | $250.00 | $7.50 | $5.75 | $13.25 |
| | | | Totals: | $53.00 |

As you can see, cashing these checks was not a good financial move. To begin with, it makes no sense to cash these checks just because they are there. Next, there is no reason why all checks should be cashed one by one. Each of the checks incurs a minimum fee of $5 or 3% of the check amount, whichever is higher.

To top it off, Erica is charged interest at the rate of 29.99% from the date the checks were cashed until the statement date, 28 days in this case. Even though Erica may have every intention to pay back these charges before the due date, the interest on these convenience checks is treated like a cash advance. Unlike the regular credit card purchases, interest on cash advances as well as most convenience checks starts counting from the day of the transaction.

Once again, when you see convenience checks, do what I do:

## Shred them or burn them!

෧෨

## Cash Advances On Credit Cards

Basically everything we described about convenience checks applies here too. Other than a serious emergency, I cannot think of any reason why you should use a cash advance on credit cards. They make no financial sense and should simply be avoided.

## Late Payments

Credit cards will charge you fees if you are late on your payments. The fees on late payments can be as high as $35. It is therefore crucial that you mark your calendar and send in your check for payment well in advance of the due date. If you send your check by post, it can sometimes take 4 days or longer to arrive. Delays with the postal service can occur especially during holidays. Getting charged extra fees just because of mail arriving one day late is painful.

More painful, because of the late payment, the credit card company can now raise your normal APR to a new penalty APR, usually 30% or higher in some cases. This new penalty APR now applies for at least six months. During this time period, you must not have another late payment before they can restore your APR back to your previous rate.

### _Think About It:_

_If you want to avoid penalty fees and penalty APRs, you may want to consider arranging an auto-payment. You can set it up with your bank or your credit card company so that each month the payment is automatically transferred from your checking account to the credit card company before the due date._

_The credit card company may suggest that you schedule only the minimum payment amount each month to avoid late fees and penalty APRs. I would strongly suggest you do what I personally do: Pay your entire monthly balance each time automatically. Yes, it takes a lot of discipline in terms of your spending habits but that's exactly the point. Knowing that you must have enough cash in your checking account for the entire balance forces you to reduce your spending._

## Calculating Interest Charges for Credit Cards

Having gone over all the reasons why you should not spend more than you can afford with your credit card, let's put some final touches on your money awareness. Let's review in detail how the credit card companies calculate interest.

The annual percentage rate (APR) is usually shown on your statement. As we learned before, the average APR in the US is 14.67% but it's usually higher for young adults and people with poor credit scores.

Credit card companies often use an average daily balance method to compute interest for each balance. This is calculated as follows:

Average Daily Balance (ADB) x Daily Periodic Rate (DPR) x # of days

ADB = Add the daily balances and divide them by the number of days in the billing period.

DPR = APR divided by 365

Let's do an example:

Say your APR is 15%, then your DPR is 15% ÷ 365 days = **0.04%**

Let us assume that your average daily balance is **$1000** and there are 28 days in your billing period. The interest is calculated like this:

### $1000 x 0.04% x 28 days = $11.20

Again, keep in mind that your APR increases the minute you make a late payment. In the example above, the penalty APR would be 29.99% and the interest would also double.

෨

## Read the Fine Print

Whether you open a bank account or get a new credit card, it always comes with the infamous fine print. The terms and conditions attached to the use of your credit card can be intimidating and they should be. Granted, a lot of this fine print is legalese and difficult to understand even for seasoned professionals. However, there are a few very important terms and conditions you have to understand. Despite the new US credit card law which came into effect in 2010, the credit card companies continue to be creative in terms of finding ways to make money from their customers. We cannot overemphasize some of these crucial points:

- Know your credit limit – know it well.
- Know your interest rate (APR) for purchases
- Know your interest rate (APR) for cash advances
- Remember that compound interest = exponential growth
- Know that penalty fees and penalty APRs apply for late payments

- Penalty APRs are much higher than your normal APR - often double
- A penalty APR will apply for at least 6 months and you cannot be late again in the same 6-month period
- Interest on cash advances is much higher than your normal APR
- Interest on penalty APRs and cash advances starts from the date of the transaction. There is no grace period as with your normal credit card purchases.

If you have not done so already, you should review your credit card in detail and note down some of these crucial terms as they apply to you.

You can find more information on the latest credit card rules along with additional insights at: www.federalreserve.gov/creditcard

∽

## Debit Cards

Debit cards are overall a better starting point when it comes to using plastic money. They work essentially the same way as writing checks or paying cash. Each time you pay with a debit card, the money is deducted from your bank account immediately. In a way, debit cards are also a better tool for you to implement a budget and restrict spending. There is no such thing as "buy it now and pay later". Using debit cards will limit your impulsive purchases immediately. You simply cannot buy today if you don't have the money in your account. You can also forget the tempting idea of buying something (you cannot afford) today thinking that you could miraculously come up with the money in a month when the credit card payment is due.

Your debit card is typically your ATM card as well; you can use it anywhere just like credit cards. Debit cards have an additional security feature. You have to enter a personal identification number (PIN) in order to use it. That also allows you to withdraw cash in addition to purchasing groceries.

Some debit cards offer rewards for frequent flyer miles or points for shopping discounts giving you similar add-on benefits like the more tempting credit cards.

There are of course a few disadvantages to note and it is (again) strongly recommended to read the fine print of your specific debit card terms. Here are some of the things to look out for:

Using a debit card for your purchases is somewhat safer from a spending perspective but these transactions are not counted towards building a good credit history. As we will learn shortly, your credit history and credit score determine the rates for all your loans and credit card terms. If you don't have an extensive credit history, a credit card might be needed to establish one. But you have to make sure to always pay your balances on time and to pay most of your balances in full. Failure to pay on time or dragging on payments too far will hurt your credit score.

Most credit card issuers offer protection for unauthorized credit card use. In case someone steals your card and goes on a spending spree, the most you would have to pay is $50. However, not all debit cards offer this kind of protection. If your debit card is stolen and a thief can get your PIN, it may be much more hassle to protect your account. You may have to prove that the card has been stolen and immediate action on your part is required to prevent additional charges or substantial loss of money.

Some debit cards allow you to spend more than you have in your bank account thereby creating an overdraft in your account. Depending on the terms, you will be charged an overdraft fee, somewhere between $20 and $30. But the banks might also charge you additional fees or interest for each day that your bank balance is negative. Make sure to check with your bank if any overdraft limits are in place and what the terms and fees are.

Above all, you must keep track of your account balances and your spending habits.

∾

## Credit Reports & FICO Scores

The three major credit reporting agencies in the US are Equifax, Experian and TransUnion. These agencies collect data on your credit history and assess your credit worthiness by assigning a credit score.

Most credit reporting agencies use a system developed by the Fair Isaac Corporation (FICO) to rate the credit worthiness of consumers. FICO scores range from 300-850; the higher your score, the better.

Higher scores have a direct impact on the terms and rates you can get on your loans. Whether you apply for a home loan, car loan or a credit card, the banks and lenders need to assess the risk they might have by lending you money. FICO scores give them a quantitative assessment of risk. Depending on your credit score, the lenders will determine how much they are prepared to lend you and at what interest rates. The higher your credit score, the more money you can borrow and the lower your interest rates for a loan. Lenders usually check all three of your FICO scores from the three major credit reporting agencies.

You may have seen numerous advertisements offering free credit reports. Be careful with those! Since most of them come with a bunch of conditions attached, in reality none of them are truly free.

As an example, a company called www.freecreditreport.com got in trouble with the regulators because their advertisements and obviously their name implied that a free credit report can be obtained from them. Unlike the name suggests www.freecreditreport.com is not a free service. A minimum charge of $1 applies when you order the report and unless you cancel within a 7-day trial period, you will be billed $14.95 each month until you cancel the account.

At the time of this writing, the only truly free credit report can be obtained through: www.annualcreditreport.com

A free credit report can be obtained once every 12 months from each of the three major credit reporting companies.

## Stolen Credit Cards & Identity Theft

Earlier, we learned that immediate action is critical if fraud is suspected on your online bank account. The same is true for lost or stolen credit cards. You should call your credit card company right away when this happens. The credit card company will suspend your current credit card and issue a new card with a new credit card number.

Equally troublesome is the growing trend of identity theft in the U.S. A regular review of your credit report and any sudden changes to your credit score may signal that someone stole your identity. Some paid services allow you to view your credit reports online and also give you alerts if a third party requests a credit report on you. They also send you alerts if there are any changes to your credit score. The cost for these services ranges between $100-$150 per year. It may be worth paying this kind of fee if you have a lot of credit card transactions, online payments or are generally concerned about the downside of having your identity stolen.

Whether you have a case of unauthorized credit card access, online security breaches or if you suspect identity theft, you should get in touch with your banks and credit card companies immediately. You should also contact the three credit bureaus and let them know about unauthorized access to your accounts, credit cards or identity theft.

The contact details for the three credit reporting agencies are:

**Equifax**
Call 800-525-6285, visit www.equifax.com
or write P.O. Box 740250 Atlanta, GA 30374

**Experian**
Call 888-397-3742, visit www.experian.com
or write P.O. Box 9556 Allen, TX 75013

**TransUnion**
Call 800-680-7289, visit www.transunion.com
or write P.O. Box 6790 Fullerton, CA 92634

Additional information about Identity Theft is provided at the following website: www.ftc.gov/bcp/edu/microsites/idtheft/

༄

## Final Notes On New Credit Card Rules

As we learned earlier, in 2010 the U.S. government enacted new rules on fees and interest charged to credit card holders. The new rules also require credit card companies to give more disclosure and warnings about the dangers of incurring too much debt.  Here is the website again where you can get more information:

www.federalreserve.gov/creditcard/

I also wanted to highlight some subtle messages within the disclosures that might still give some wrong impressions if you don't fully grasp the concept of compound interest and the time value of money. A good example is the new rule requiring credit card companies to show how long it will take you to pay off your balance if you only make the minimum payments. They also need to make a comparison showing how much you need to pay if you wanted to pay off the entire amount in say three years.

Let's use the example directly from the official website. If you owe $3,000 and your interest rate is 14.4%, your credit card statement might show the following disclosure:

| New balance | $3,000.00 |
|---|---|
| Minimum payment due | $90.00 |
| Payment due date | 4/20/12 |

**Late Payment Warning:** If we do not receive your minimum payment by the date listed above, you may have to pay a $35 late fee and your APRs may be increased up to the Penalty APR of 28.99%.

**Minimum Payment Warning:** If you make only the minimum payment each period, you will pay more in interest and it will take you longer to pay off your balance. For example:

| If you make no additional charges using this card and each month you pay... | You will pay off the balance shown on this statement in about... | And you will end up paying an estimated total of... |
|---|---|---|
| Only the minimum payment | 11 years | $4,745 |
| $103 | 3 years | $3,712 (Savings = $1,033) |

While these disclosures are an important step in the right direction, this new government rule falls short of an additional warning that should be much stronger. Clearly, it is better to pay more than the minimum amount each month as it would help you pay off the debt much faster. However, notice the subtle word **"Savings"** in the last row. Let me make this crystal clear for you: **Always pay off your credit card debt in full every month!**

Yes, paying off slightly more than the minimum amount is better than paying only the bare minimum but it's still making the credit card companies way too much money far too easily. Instead, it is costing YOU the credit card holder a small fortune in interest expenses.

> ### Reality Check:
> You <u>DO NOT</u> save by paying anything less than the full payment on a credit card but you may make the credit card company a little less money by paying a slightly higher amount than the minimum payment. Still, the credit card companies would rather you pay them in incremental amounts. As attractive as it may sound (savings), you are better off facing the music now rather than later.
>
> **"Savings" is a term that should only be used when it applies, as in the money you have in your savings account.**

∾

## Gift Cards & Prepaid Debit Cards

Gift cards and prepaid debit cards have become increasingly popular. These little plastic gifts have turned into a multi-billion dollar industry. You can get gift cards from all kinds of retailers just about anywhere. These types of cards are very convenient indeed. Say you need to get a present for a friend but really don't know what to get. Gift cards are the easy way out, less worrying about what to buy, just select an amount and you're set. Here's the problem though...

In reality, gift cards are cash but with certain conditions attached. Although I love iTunes, you can't buy groceries with an iTunes card. Same goes for other retailers; they restrict you to use your cash only at certain places. There's also a bit of a trap with these cards. When we buy something with a gift card we often have a small amount remaining on the card, say $1.39. Unless you are disciplined and make a conscious effort to remember, you're more than likely going to tuck that card away somewhere and forget about it. Some people even go as far as throwing them

away after a while, thinking the few cents aren't worth going back to that store. It is exactly that attitude which is giving U.S. retailers several billion Dollars in uncollected balances, an easy way for companies to make money from your neglect.

Onto something even more annoying: **Prepaid Debit Cards**.

One of the biggest traps these days are prepaid debit cards. Although the government issued new rules in 2010, giving consumers more protection, the issuers of these cards continue to find ways to charge fees for these cards.

Expiration dates for some of these cards have to be at least 5 years, but if you kept a balance on a card for say one year, the card issuer can often charge monthly service fees. In one case, a friend of mine had been given a Visa gift card and hadn't used it for a year only to realize that there was a $2.50 monthly reoccurring service charge that ate up most of his balance. That was a nasty surprise when he eventually tried using the card.

The most appalling fee however, which is still perfectly legal by the way, is an activation fee that is charged when you first use the card. I have just recently seen an activation fee of $4.95 for a $25 gift card. That's almost 20% right off the top which in my humble opinion is completely unethical. Granted, there are restrictions on some of the many other fees these banks used to get away with. It still kills me how a 20% activation fee can be legal.

**My advice in all this:** Prepare a self-made gift, something of real inherent value and stay away from those ridiculous and impersonal money sucking gadgets called gift cards. If your friends and relatives ask you what you want for your birthday or for the holidays, ask them to contribute to your savings account. That's a much better proposition that will help you later on when we learn how to implement your budget and establish your first financial plan.

## Loans & Mortgages

### Loans in General
Before the arrival of credit cards, most people financed their purchases via loans and credit lines if they did not have the cash to pay for something up front.

Loans were meant for larger purchases such as big equipment, cars and homes. Today, car loans and home loans make up the bulk of personal loans. But retailers have been finding new ways to attract customers by offering financing for smaller purchases including electronics and musical instruments. The most aggressive retailers offer 0% financing for certain limited time periods. Those types of financing deals have been used by car dealers, home furnishing retailers, electronics retailers and others to attract buyers. Some retailers entice you to spend using advertising slogans such as: "Make no payments for 12 months."

Before we take a closer look at some of the basic financing options, realize that hundreds of books have been written on the subject of loans and mortgages. We can only cover some of the basic elements and give you a rough overview of what you need to be aware of.

## Car Loans

No matter what type of car you might get, it is presumably one of your larger purchases. Since a lot of money is involved, it definitely pays to do your homework and shop around for good offers. Car dealers know that of course and they make every effort to get you in the door by bombarding you with seemingly unbeatable offers.

Once you're inside a car dealership, you're bombarded again with financing deals. Those car loans can be tricky and you should be careful with some of the more alluring ones such as 0% financing.

First off, know that car salesmen are often making more money from the financing of your car rather than from sales commissions. As a result, the incentive is to tempt you into taking on more debt because that provides them with a larger commission.

Zero percent financing has been a major success for car dealerships. But you need to be aware of a few things before considering these types of deals:

- Realize that you will need a good credit history and a close to perfect credit score to qualify for zero percent financing. Most of the 0% financing offers would only apply to consumers with a credit score above 750 and closer to 800 (850 being the max. credit score). As you may realize, very few people would qualify for such a high score.

- Suppose your credit score is close to 800 and you do qualify for zero percent financing, you should still watch out. Car dealers and car salesmen still like to maximize their returns on each deal. When they cannot make enough money from the financing of your car, they need to make up the commission income elsewhere. As a result, they will play hard ball when it comes to the actual sales price. While you might be excited about the zero percent financing, make sure you still get a reasonable purchase price for the car.

- Zero percent financing does NOT mean no payments. In fact, the monthly payments on a 0% interest car loan are often higher than your typical low interest car loan. Unlike an average car loan with is about 3-4 years in length, zero percent financing deals have shorter terms usually not more than two years. This means you would have to pay back the entire loan in only 24 installments, albeit without interest. Only if you can afford much higher monthly payments would such a deal make sense.

- The biggest potential issues have to do with the fine print again. If you are late on a payment just once, the sweet 0% financing goes out the window. Now the terms of the contract revert to a typical loan with much higher interest rates. Rest assured that there might be some additional penalties and late payment fees too. Most frustrating however is the fact that you will have to pay the higher interest from the beginning of the loan. Imagine if you made a late payment on the 21st installment of a two year (24 month) zero percent financing agreement. That would indeed be a rough deal requiring you to pay back the interest as if it had accumulated for 21 months.

Before you sign your name on the dotted line, read the fine print very carefully. You have to be comfortable with higher monthly payments but you also need to be disciplined enough to make every payment on time. If you have any doubts about being able to meet all payments on time, consider another way of reducing your overall purchase price, perhaps with a generous cash back offer.

Let's look at a direct comparison between a 3-year car loan at 5% with a 10% cash-back versus a 0% financing arrangement. Suppose you bought a new car costing $30,000 and you qualify for a 0% financing option. Here are the numbers:

| Car Loan | 0% Loan |
|---|---|
| Loan Amount | $30,000.00 |
| Length (months) | 24 |
| Monthly Payment | $1,250.00 |
| Total Interest | $0.00 |
| Cash Back | $0.00 |
| **Total Cost of Car** | **$30,000.00** |

| Car Loan | 5% Loan |
|---|---|
| Loan Amount | $27,000.00 |
| Length (months) | 36 |
| Monthly Payment | $809.21 |
| Total Interest | $2,131.71 |
| Cash Back | $3,000.00 |
| **Total Cost of Car** | **$29,131.71** |

Granted you would have to get the car loan with your bank to be able to qualify for the cash back discount from the car manufacturer, but the example emphasizes the point that you should carefully evaluate all options with your financial transactions. What may appear to be the best offer on first glance could easily turn into a much costlier deal than you would have expected.

To give you an idea of the numbers, if you were to default or in case you were late on a payment, your accumulated interest could easily be $3,000 per year (that's only at a rate of 10% per annum) or higher. Again, make sure you read and understand the fine print. It can save you plenty of headaches and lots of money.

### Think About It:
*Taking advantage of discounts, incentives and sales offers are indeed an important way to minimize spending and it does pay to compare various offers in detail. Here's another thought though: If something needs massive advertising and huge incentives to be sold maybe it isn't such a good product after all. In other words, if there is a product you really need and want, granted that product is of high quality and a good quality brand name, are all these incentives really needed? The best test is to ask yourself if you would still buy the product if it wasn't on sale. If your main rationale for buying that product is based on incentives and discounts, then you should re-evaluate whether the product is right for you.*

The example of a car loan can easily be applied to all other financing arrangements be it home furnishings, appliances or any of your professional equipment. If someone offers you a 0% financing deal on a new drum set for instance, carefully consider the downside and take some time to read and understand the terms of the financing offer.

As we will learn in the upcoming chapter, certain types of products like electronics and typical consumer products have a very poor resale value. You may have heard the phrase that your new car loses 10% of its value the minute you drive it off the lot. A similar case applies to most consumer products and also to a large chunk of professional equipment and electronics that we accumulate over the years. If you factor in the financing cost for your equipment, realize that this only exacerbates the poor resale value.

# Mortgages

Very few people have enough money to pay for a home with cash. Nearly every home buyer has to take on a loan to finance the purchase of a house. These types of loans are called mortgages. Mortgages are similar to car loans and other personal loans but they are usually for much larger amounts and the payments are structured for longer time periods. Common mortgages last 15, 20 or 30 years.

Since purchasing a home and taking on a mortgage presents the largest financial transaction for the great majority of all people, it makes sense to carefully consider all options and fully understand the loan terms before taking on such large amounts of debt.

### How Mortgages Work

Unless you can find a willing friend or relative you will be hard pressed to get an unsecured loan from a bank today. This is true for most loans, especially for mortgages. Banks will ask you to provide some security in form of collateral in case you were to default on the loan.

In a typical mortgage, the home buyer pledges the property as collateral and the bank has a lien or claim on that property. The same applies to car loans by the way. Banks hold the title (a legal certificate of ownership) of your car until your car loan is fully paid off.

If you bought a house with a mortgage and you were to stop making payments on the loan, you could be in default. The bank would then initiate a foreclosure, claim the house as its property and sell it to clear the debt.

Using the property as collateral however, is not enough security for the bank extending the loan. Most home buyers have to come up with a sizeable down payment before a bank is willing to finance the purchase of a house. The amount of the down payment depends on a number of factors including your credit score and overall credit history, your current income, the level of any other debts you currently have, the price of the house, the location and a few other economic factors.

A typical mortgage might require you to come up with a down payment of 20% of the purchase price of the house.

## Think About It:

*The US mortgage crisis opened the eyes of many unassuming home buyers. The notion that property prices can only go up was a rather naïve assumption. The level of debts most home buyers took on was far too high. In exceptional cases, some people took on mortgages with no down payment. Those and some other types of loans are extremely risky evident in the highest foreclosure rates the U.S. has ever experienced.*

*In the years 2002-2007, credit standards have been relaxed and many of the important credit requirements have basically been ignored. This led to a large number of people qualifying for home loans that would never have qualified under the traditional credit standards. Today, banks and mortgage lenders have become extremely strict and upped their credit standards substantially, which is a good thing. Unless you have an excellent credit score and above average finances, you will need a down payment of 20% or more to obtain a mortgage. Some banks today require down payments of 40% or more for customers with less than perfect credit.*

## Calculating Mortgage Payments

Calculating the exact mortgage payments is a bit more difficult than your normal compound interest calculations. You will need a financial calculator or spreadsheet to calculate the exact monthly payment and to view the entire schedule of payments.

Here is a typical mortgage situation:

Suppose a house costs $300,000 and you want to get a mortgage to buy that house. The Bank requires a down payment of 20%.

**Purchase Price:**  $300,000.00
**Down Payment:**  $60,000.00  *(= 300,000 x 20%)*
**Loan Amount:**  $240,000.00

To calculate the monthly payment we need to know a few more things, namely the length of the loan in years and the interest rate the bank charges for the loan. Suppose the following terms are given by the bank:

**Loan Amount:**  $240,000.00
**Interest Rate:**  5%
**Lengths in years:**  30
**Monthly Payment:**  $1,288.37

To calculate the monthly payment, we need the following formula:

$$M = P \times J \div [\, 1-(1+J)^{-N}\,]$$

P = Principal or loan amount
J = Monthly interest; in our case $5\% \div 12 = 0.42\%$
N = Number of months of the loan; in our case $30 \times 12 = 360$

You can do this calculation with either a financial calculator or with spreadsheets like Excel, Open Office or Google Docs. When you use spreadsheets, you can go one step further and produce the entire payment schedule. Below is an example of how the first year of payments for this 30 year loan would look like:

Loan Repayment Schedule

| Month | Starting Balance | Interest | Principal Paid | New Balance |
|-------|------------------|----------|----------------|-------------|
| 1 | 240,000.00 | 1,000.00 | 288.37 | 239,711.63 |
| 2 | 239,711.63 | 998.80 | 289.57 | 239,422.05 |
| 3 | 239,422.05 | 997.59 | 290.78 | 239,131.27 |
| 4 | 239,131.27 | 996.38 | 291.99 | 238,839.28 |
| 5 | 238,839.28 | 995.16 | 293.21 | 238,546.07 |
| 6 | 238,546.07 | 993.94 | 294.43 | 238,251.64 |
| 7 | 238,251.64 | 992.72 | 295.66 | 237,955.99 |
| 8 | 237,955.99 | 991.48 | 296.89 | 237,659.10 |
| 9 | 237,659.10 | 990.25 | 298.13 | 237,360.97 |
| 10 | 237,360.97 | 989.00 | 299.37 | 237,061.61 |
| 11 | 237,061.61 | 987.76 | 300.62 | 236,760.99 |
| 12 | 236,760.99 | 986.50 | 301.87 | 236,459.12 |

ﺀﻮ

## Loans & Mortgage Calculators

There are literally hundreds free online tools and calculators allowing you to compute loans and mortgages of all kinds. Just do an online search to find some of these tools.

If you are familiar with spreadsheets, you are welcome to use our simple loan calculator. It can be downloaded from resource site (see back section of the book).

If you have never used spreadsheets before, the following sites can give you some useful tips to get you started:

**Google Spreadsheets** *(free online spreadsheet – part of Google Docs)*
http://tinyurl.com/lpw299

**Open Office** *(free downloadable version similar to Microsoft Office)*
http://tinyurl.com/z4bvx

**Microsoft Excel** *(Part of Microsoft Office)*
http://tinyurl.com/287cgww

## Other Important Factors To Consider

Most first-time buyers make one common mistake: They under-estimate the substantial financial commitment of a home purchase. It is easy to forget many of the costs and hassles in addition to the monthly mortgage payments. Property taxes, home insurance and other property related insurances, utilities, repairs & maintenance as well as upgrades and more furnishings increase the overall monthly expense of living significantly. As a general rule, I like to budget an amount equal to the monthly mortgage payment to pay for all these additional expenses. In our example of a $240,000 loan with a monthly payment of $1,288, budget at least another $1,200 in additional expenses to have a safety cushion in case you are hit with unexpected repairs, property taxes or insurance premiums.

You should also have an extra 6 months of savings to pay for mortgage and other expenses, just in case you might lose your job.

## Final Thoughts On Loans & Debt

Traditionally, banks and lenders gave credit and made loans to consumers based on a number of criteria. These criteria are sometimes called the **4 C's of Credit**. The four criteria are:

- Character
- Capacity
- Capital
- Collateral

Each of these words implies a set of rules for the evaluation and risk management procedures banks undertake before extending a loan. In simple terms, a lender wants to know who you are, what your track record was with regard to paying back previous loans, what your finances look like and what types of security you can provide in case your financial circumstances were to change. Fair enough, if you were to loan money to a stranger, you too would want to make sure that you're getting paid back.

I would like you to think of these evaluation criteria from a different perspective. If a bank has some reservations about lending you money, you should really consider whether it makes sense for you to take on so much debt. Think of the banks evaluation measures as a gauge for your personal debt burden. Not all debt is bad, but too much debt can lead to a financial nightmare.

# FIVE

## *Making Money Work For You*

### Once More: The Time Value Of Money

In chapter two, we first learned about the time value of money. When it comes to finance, we all have to make a choice between something of value (i.e. cash or investments) and time - we cannot have both. We either spend our money now or we save and spend it later. If we wait and spend our money later, we naturally want to be compensated for giving up the pleasure of instant gratification now. In essence, any money that is saved or invested should provide us some benefit in the future.

### Measuring Future Benefits

When we speak of time value of money we associate it with the need for money or investments to grow over time. That concept is most elegantly expressed in the form of interest or return on money invested.

Using just a simple example, if you invest $100 for one year and that investment is valued at $110 at the end of the first year, you would have a return of 10% on your investment. The $10 gain compared with your initial investment of $100 is expressed as a 10% return.

You can calculate this in a couple of formats:

    a) **($110 ÷ $100) – 1    = 0.1 or 10%**

    b) **($110 - $100) ÷ 100 = 0.1 or 10%**

◦◦

## Why Saving Is Important

The U.S. experienced many periods of economic booms but also the bust cycles that usually follow economic expansion. The recession of 2008/2009 was one of the worst in U.S. history. As it happens during these cycles, the government tries to stimulate the economy and interest rates can drop to very low levels. When interest rates are at record low levels such as the years 2009 and 2010, the time value of money hardly makes a dent in the short term. However, we should not ignore the longer term impact and the high likelihood that interest rates can go higher. Higher interest rates would give more of an incentive to save and achieve some returns for instance from basic savings accounts and CDs.

Yet, no matter where interest rates might be at a given time, you need a financial safety cushion. That cushion is extra important for you dear reader, and here's why:

Self-employed persons such as musicians, artists and young adults without steady or full-time jobs have inconsistent flows of income.

Say you're a musician and you might land a great gig and go on tour for three months earning say $2,500 a week. But there might be a break of three months or more before the next gig materializes. What can you do in the meantime to earn a living?

If you're lucky you might be able to teach (although most students would rather have a steady instructor or someone who can teach every week). Being out of town for three months closes a lot of doors and you have to be prepared that some of the income generating jobs and gigs might not be there when you are back from a tour. The best way to deal with a situation like this is to get financially prepared. You should deposit a large chunk of the income from the tour into a savings account. That can provide a safety net for the time when no money is coming in. If you were on tour 6 months per year, make sure you have at least six months of living expenses saved up just to be on the safe side.

Here's another example:

Say you're a song writer and you just had an offer to write the music for a film project. Due to the poor economic situation, all film and television budgets are running at a bare minimum. The producer offers neither up-front payments nor any allowances until the project is completed in about four months. You would absolutely love to do this project which is incredibly challenging but it allows you to collaborate with some of the best talents in the industry.

To make a long story short, this could be your decisive career move that requires 100% of your attention. There is no way you could take on any other side job if you wanted this project to turn out perfectly.

Can you afford to take on this project without getting paid for four months?

If you are an average musician the answer is probably "no." In fact, this is not just a dilemma for musicians and artists. The average U.S. worker has less than three months' worth of living expenses saved up. Hence the phrase: "Living from pay check to pay check."

# The Essential Savings Goal

Let's get our savings plan started with a goal in mind - that is a dollar amount we want to reach. The amount is different for each of us but we can still set a savings goal.

My personal rule in terms of a savings goal is:

> ***Save at least one year's worth of living expenses.***

This rule does not just apply to musicians and artists but to anyone who is serious about his/her financial well-being. In fact, before I consider giving investment advice to clients, I would tell them the same: .

> **Don't dabble in the financial markets until you reach your essential savings goal!**

Having enough savings to last an entire year might sound like an impossible goal at first, but rather than throw in the towel at the beginning, remember that you can attack this goal from several angles. The key to success is simply based on the concept of **"living within your means."**

We will learn more about ways to save money and establishing a budget in the next chapter. For now, just remember that you can get to your goal much faster by attacking both sides of the equation:

Increase your monthly income **and** decrease your monthly expenses at the same time!

### Investing: A Preview

So investing is out until we have some serious money saved up. But while we are working on a plan to get above the investing threshold, let's take a peek at some of the possible investment options.

When people think of investing, their first thought might be investing in stocks. But there are many other ways to invest. You might be surprised to learn about some of my own favorite investment choices.

I like to think of investing as a way of **making money work for you** and there are many ways that can be done. Stocks, bonds or property are examples of the many investment choices out there. These choices are often grouped into similar types called asset classes. Bonds represent an asset class for instance.

# What Are Assets?

<u>Assets</u> are considered things that you <u>own</u> as opposed to <u>liabilities</u> which are things that you <u>owe</u>.

When it comes to investing, assets are things that you buy in the hope of generating some financial benefit in the future. The financial benefit can take different forms. A benefit could be as simple as the interest on your savings account or as complex as the pay-out from investments in complex derivatives. An asset is therefore a vehicle that enables your money to work for you.

## Types of Assets

The typical financial assets include stocks, bonds, CDs, savings accounts etc. We will learn more about these types of financial assets in our final chapter.

In addition to financial assets there are physical assets as well. For instance, a house that you own is an asset providing a number of benefits, mainly in the form of shelter and giving you a home to live. This type of asset doesn't come cheap. The cost of owning this asset can sometimes outweigh the benefits. For instance, if you bought a house during times of a real estate bubble, as was the case in 2002-2007, your benefits from that asset might only be a rather expensive roof over your head. But suppose you bought a house in 1995 when property prices were relatively inexpensive. The financial benefit of the asset would then be the increase in the market price of the house.

There are many other physical assets such as cars, furniture, gadgets or musical instruments. These physical assets can also go up and down in value. For the most part however, the prices of physical assets which are used in your daily life slowly depreciate over time.

There is yet another type of asset class which is neither considered a financial asset nor a physical asset. In accounting this type of asset is called "good will." Good will could be a (famous) brand name, a logo and often the reputation of a company or a person.

> ### *Think About It:*
> *The names and logos of famous companies like Coca Cola, McDonalds or Apple carry a high value, albeit financial experts often disagree on how to assess that value. Nevertheless, consider what happens to the stock price of a company when it experiences difficulties with its reputation. In early 2010, the car manufacturer Toyota, had problems with numerous recalls and safety concerns. As a result, the company's stock price dropped about 20% in a matter of just a few weeks. That implies a loss of value in the tens of billions of dollars in stock market valuation. Although some experts might disagree on the exact value of assets such as reputation, one can clearly see that these types of assets can definitely impact the financial well-being of an organization.*

While some types of assets are difficult to measure, there are ways in which you can invest in these assets. To name a few:

- Investing in education
- Investing in skills
- Investing in reputation (doing things right)

## My Best Investment Ever

No, it was not some amazing stock trade nor was it an exceptional business deal. The best investment I ever made was the investment in my education. Going to school, learning new skills and continuously re-investing in a lifelong learning process was the single best investment choice for me. That choice continues to provide the most substantial pay-off of all my investments. Those hard to measure assets such as skills, talents and know-how are assets that do not easily decline in value. Instead, with time and more experience your skills become more refined and provide a bigger return on your initial investment. But make no mistake, just like any other type of investment in financial assets, you have to keep an eye on it and re-invest some of your returns to upgrade and enhance your skills. It will allow you to better keep up with the economic trends and the market forces in your industry.

When it comes to your personal finances, you have already done an important first step towards investing in your own education just by purchasing and reading this book. The next step is to practice and implement what you have learned.

> ### *Think About It:*
> *Say you were the only actor in town with a unique deep voice that can make an entire audience shiver just by listening to it. That would be a great asset especially for voice-overs. During times when thrillers and horror movies are in great demand, your phone would be ringing off the hook with opportunities to derive a substantial financial benefit from your unique skill.*
>
> *Another example could include the craft and talent of a song writer or composer. As a composer you would invest many hours and lots of efforts in coming up with new song material that could be either recorded or licensed for TV and Film.*
>
> *Investing time, effort and money in learning and improving these skills should also be considered as "investing in assets." Although these assets are not easily measured, they can provide a huge financial benefit, possibly the biggest benefit of all your investments.*

## Appreciation & Depreciation

As we discovered earlier, assets are things that you own. The price or the value of some of these assets can go up or down. When an asset goes up in value, it is called appreciation. When it goes down in value it is subject to depreciation.

A good example for depreciation would be a car. When you buy a new car it loses on average 11% of its value the minute you drive it off the lot[26].

In terms of car depreciation, take a look at how a car loses most of its value within the first few years. After 5 years, an average car is only worth 40% of its original purchase price.

---

26 Source: www.edmunds.com

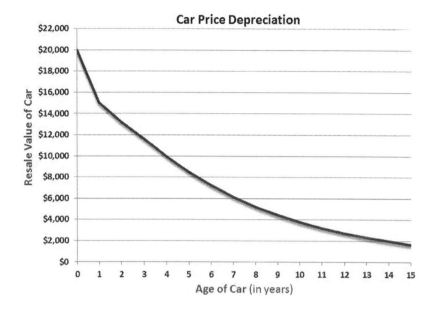

**Car Price Depreciation**

Source: http://www.carprice.com/depreciation-calculator

A similar argument could be made with everyday items such as appliances, furniture, electronics and gadgets. These days, it is very easy to find the value of almost anything you own. Just go online to websites like eBay or Craigslist to find out what other people would be willing to pay for used items like ovens, refrigerators, iPods, etc.

The prices of electronics are prone to bigger price drops, often losing 50% of their original purchase price within the first year. The reason for the much faster price depreciation in electronics is based on the speed of technological advances. As new technologies develop, older systems are often rendered useless. Prime examples are computers and communications equipment.

For your amusement, I'd like to share an example of a steep price decline of an electronic piece of equipment. In late 1989, I bought a digital reverb for a whopping $2,000, which was a lot of money back then. Here is a photo of this master piece of technology in those days.

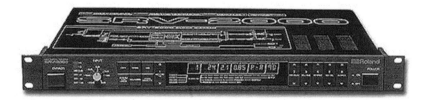

Recently, I saw the exact same model on eBay selling for an earth-shattering $12.50. After about 20 years, that piece of equipment (which

I still own by the way and which is still in pristine condition) is now worth a mere 0.625% of the original price. Take it from me and learn from my money mistakes. Certain types of assets are not meant to keep their value over a long period of time.

But it's not all bad out there. Some types of assets can retain their value, even increase multifold over a course of a few decades. Enter the hall of fame of musical instruments and let's look at one of the most popular electric guitars of all time, the Fender Stratocaster.

The list price of a Fender Stratocaster in 1954 was $250, quite a lot of money for that time period too. Let's say you had bought such a guitar in 1954, or shall we say your grandparents did? Assuming that guitar is still in good condition, it can easily be sold on eBay for $50,000 or more – a true collector's item.

Let's do the math on this and compare it to a financial investment, say an investment in stocks over the same time period.

Buying the asset (Fender Strat) in 1954 @     **$250**
Selling the asset (Fender Strat) in 2010 @     **$50,000**
Net profit from investment =     **$49,750**

Average rate of return over 56 years:     **370%**
Annualized compounded rate of return since 1954:     **approx. 10%**

Compare that with investing in stocks:

Stock market compounded rate of return since 1954:     **approx. 7%**

You may not realize it now but this type of investment return beats most of the highly paid fund managers. To achieve such a high appreciation in the price of an asset you have to search long and hard.

We can also draw a few conclusions from this:

Certain assets are more prone to depreciate than others. As much as possible you should balance the need for any purchases, be it musical equipment, electronics or other assets, with the prospects for future price values. Know that electronics and mass-produced items tend to lose value faster.

> ### *Think About It:*
> *The attraction of having the latest electronic gadget is often very tempting. You might feel compelled to get that latest must-have item as soon as possible. But you should seriously consider the fast price depreciation of these gadgets. Unless you absolutely need a particular electronic product to perform a job today, consider buying the product in six months when you can possibly get the same thing at half the price.*

## Things to Remember

- Minimize impulse shopping for gadgets
- Assess resale value of your professional equipment
- Assess if additional equipment provides extra income
- Establish needs versus wants for your business and career
- Maintain your equipment and instruments to increase resale value

We will revisit these points and additional money saving tips when we discuss Budgeting and Planning – coming up next.

# SIX

## *Budgeting & Planning*

### What Is A Budget?

Budgets are made all the time. Governments, companies, charities, sports clubs, unions, even churches establish budgets to deal with their finances. People establish their own personal budgets too.

While most governments and larger organizations look at budgets primarily as a spending plan, I prefer to look at a personal budget this way:

**A budget is a plan that guides you to live within your means.**

Living within your means is the key to your financial well-being. As long as you spend less than you make, you will get financially ahead.

Although many people establish budgets, we must question how realistic some of these budgets are. The fact that very few people can manage to save and get financially ahead implies that they either did not implement a budget or that they abandoned their budget at some point. The same could be said for some companies and for most government organizations that are notorious for spending more than they earn.

Once again, the only way to get financially ahead is to spend less than you earn or as financially smart people say:

**"It's not what you make but what you keep!"**

To get a glimpse of how money can be your best friend one day and your worst enemy the next, just do a Google search for *famous bankruptcies* or *bankrupt musicians*. You will get a list of names that rivals any guest list at a red carpet Hollywood event. Among the more popular musicians with money problems you can find:

- Meat Loaf (filed bankruptcy in 1983; $1.6 million in debt)
- Jerry Lee Lewis (filed bankruptcy in 1988; $3 million in debt)
- TLC (filed bankruptcy in 1995; debts of $3.5 million)
- Toni Braxton ($3.9 million in debt)
- MC Hammer ($13.7 million in debt)
- Willie Nelson (owed the I.R.S. $16.7 million)
- Billy Joel (went bankrupt three times)

There are many more; but the most shocking evidence of poor money management is the sad story of the late Michael Jackson.

> **"Jackson racked up about $500 million of debt, according to sources cited by the Wall Street Journal"**[27]

> ***Think About It:***
> *The lives of the rich and famous are usually plastered all over the media. Seeing images of big stars surrounded by luxury, who wouldn't be envious of some of the perks of that lifestyle - fair enough!*
>
> *Yet, what most people forget, the rules of finance apply to the big stars just as they apply to you and me. A famous musician, movie star or athlete could make millions in one year only to lose it all the next year if he or she isn't careful with the way money is spent. Remember: It's not what you make...*

Poor money management skills are not limited to musicians. Famous artists, movie stars, athletes and even some businessmen had to appear in bankruptcy courts. Their money problems were not primarily caused by an inability to make money. They all made plenty of it, often tens of millions each year. But when you spend more than you make, you still end up with a minus sign on your bank balance.

With that in mind, let's learn how to budget.

༺༻

## Creating Your First Budget

Before we even consider fitting some numbers into our budget, we need to go on a fact finding mission. Let's take the Weight Watcher's approach to getting a grip on your personal finances.

## Phase 1: Finding The Facts

Budgets are often established based on some preconceived notions as to what income and expenses should look like. Too many budgets have

---

27 Reuters, Fri Jun 26, 2009, http://tinyurl.com/27wrgsd

been abandoned because of unrealistic assumptions. In order to create a realistic and sustainable budget, our first step is to find out exactly where our money comes from and what we spend it on.

Figuring out our income is relatively easy. The spending is the tricky part and that is where we should put our emphasis on. Fact finding in finance is no different from fact finding for weight watchers. You have to be brutally honest with yourself otherwise your numbers won't reflect reality and your budget will be useless. You won't be able to trim down your financial weight (your expenses).

So our first step in creating a budget is to write down every single expense on a daily basis - and I mean every single expense. From the coffee you bought at Starbucks to the newspaper you bought at the news stand. Every penny counts whether you spend it with cash, your credit card, debit card or check. You also have to include the bigger ticket items such as rent, utilities, insurances, etc.

To keep a tab of your daily expenses you can use a simple spending diary as seen below.

| What did I spend my money on? | How much? |
| --- | --- |
| Breakfast | $3.00 |
| Gasoline | $40.00 |
| Lunch | $6.95 |
| Coffee | $4.00 |
| Groceries | $30.00 |
| Drinks | $12.00 |
| **Daily Total:** | **$95.95** |

Make sure to keep this diary up-to-date and record every single expense. A good way to turn this into a habit is to combine it with another daily routine, like brushing your teeth. If you can recall what your daily expenses were, jot them down. Better yet, keep receipts of everything and add up all the numbers. This should not take more than a couple of minutes, about the same time it takes to brush your teeth. Follow this routine for at least a month to get a good overview of all your expenses.

Those of you who are already good at keeping track may want to go one step further. In addition to just writing down the expenses, you can also categorize the expense items. We will go over this in detail shortly, but for now, think of major categories that your expenses could be grouped into. You can start with just a few basic categories while we are still in our fact-finding phase. Categories will be extremely helpful in our budgeting and planning efforts. A spending diary with a few basic expense categories would look like this:

| What did I spend my money on? | How much? |
|---|---|
| Breakfast (Food/Groceries) | $3.00 |
| Gasoline (Transportation) | $40.00 |
| Lunch (Food/Groceries) | $6.95 |
| Coffee (Food/Groceries) | $4.00 |
| Groceries (Food/Groceries) | $30.00 |
| Drinks (Entertainment) | $12.00 |
| | |
| **Daily Total:** | **$95.95** |

## Phase 2:  Analyze Your Expenses

Assuming that you were honest and diligent at tracking all your expenses, you may have had your first "aha" moment already. Although we all intuitively know what we spend our money on, it's yet another story to see the totals right in front of you. Most people are shocked when they realize where their money goes.

Phase two therefore begins with analyzing the data we collected for a whole month. Now is also a good time to firm up your expense categories. Although there are no strict rules as to what these categories should be, here are a few often used categories you could follow:

**Housing, Food/Groceries, Transportation, Debt/Obligations, Personal & Health, Education, Entertainment, Miscellaneous, Savings.**

Choose the categories that fit your lifestyle and make sense to you.  Also, remember that categories are just labels. They can easily be changed to meet your personal preference.

An important aspect of your analysis is how you look at the data. To get a good overview, add up all the totals for the categories and create a summary sheet showing the amounts of each category as well as your total expenses. Sound complicated? Then let's do an example.

In our earlier example, we had listed the expenses in a simple format and added a few categories along with each expense item. Adding up the totals for each category can be done by using different color check marks. Once you entered each item in your calculator, check it off with a color pen like this:

| **What did I spend my money on?** | **How much?** |
|---|---|
| Breakfast (Food/Groceries) | $3.00 |
| Gasoline (Transportation) | $40.00 |
| Lunch (Food/Groceries) | $6.95 |
| Coffee (Food/Groceries) | $4.00 |
| Groceries (Food/Groceries) | $30.00 |
| Drinks (Entertainment) | $12.00 |
| **Daily Total:** | **$95.95** |

Adding up the amounts in the "Food/Groceries" category gives you a total of $43.95. From our previous example, we know that the total of all expenses was $95.95. To get the percentage of the total expenses, divide $43.95 by $95.95 which is 0.4581 or 45.81%.

Do the same thing for the other categories and you will get the following overall results:

- Food/Groceries:     $43.95  or 45.81% of total expenses
- Transportation:     $40.00  or 41.69% of total expenses
- Entertainment:      $12.00  or 12.51% of total expenses

This method works fine with just a few expenses and only a few categories as part of our mini example. You can imagine though, in a realistic exercise for a whole month, it may not be the most efficient method to use. Let's look at some alternatives.

**The Low-Tech Option**
Suppose we use the same expense categories we looked at earlier:

Get some standard letter envelopes and write the name of a category on each of the envelopes. These envelopes represent our categories for expense tracking. On a daily basis gather all the receipts, bills and invoices. Sort them and place them into the envelope meant for each category. For expense items without any receipts, use a small sheet similar to our basic spending diary form and add the expense items on that list. Keep collecting receipts for the entire tracking period. At the end of say four weeks, you can then add up all expense items in each category to see the totals. In a simple low-tech format, you can write the result on the envelope or on a separate sheet of paper if you wish. Finally, you will need to add the totals for each category to arrive at an overall monthly expense amount.

In our mini-example with only three categories it would look like this:

Food/Groceries    Transportation    Entertainment    Total Expenses

         $

$43.95            $40.00            $12.00            $95.95

### Think About It:

*The envelope method might sound antiquated but there are some very practical reasons why this method is useful. Think of April 15th, the much dreaded dead- line for completing your tax returns. Keeping up this low-tech method during the year will come in handy when it comes to preparing your taxes. If you have certain expenses pertaining to your business or your personal taxes, you can group them within the appropriate envelopes. Come tax day, your work will be much easier in finishing a tax return, having the relevant expenses already sorted and added up.*

*Another advantage of this method lies in its flexibility. You can easily re-categorize everything. If you consider adding new categories, just get another envelope and start putting your expense items into the envelope as needed.*

### Still Low-Tech But More Efficient

Suppose we use the same categories we can now enter our expenses in a handy table format. This format provides an easy-to-grasp overview of all your expenses based on each category. The expenses from our mini-example would look like this:

| Expense: | Housing | Food & Groceries | Transport | Debt & Obligations | Personal & Health | Education | Entertain | Misc. |
|---|---|---|---|---|---|---|---|---|
| Breakfast | | 3.00 | | | | | | |
| Gasoline | | | 40.00 | | | | | |
| Lunch | | 6.95 | | | | | | |
| Coffee | | 4.00 | | | | | | |
| Groceries | | 30.00 | | | | | | |
| Drinks | | | | | | | 12.00 | |
| Totals: | | $43.95 | $40.00 | | | | $12.00 | |

On our resource site, you can download a blank version of this sheet, as well as other preformatted sheets including the easy to use spending diary.

# The Spreadsheet Approach

Before going out and buying one of the many personal finance software applications, consider using a spreadsheet to handle your personal finances.

We briefly looked at spreadsheets in chapter four. To get a better understanding, you may wish to review the primers of the three main spreadsheet applications again.

Google Spreadsheets:    **http://tinyurl.com/lpw299**

Open Office:    **http://tinyurl.com/z4bvx**

Microsoft Excel:    **http://tinyurl.com/287cgww**

Microsoft Excel is currently the most sophisticated spreadsheet application. However, it is fairly expensive and is usually sold as part of Microsoft Office. Unless you have Microsoft Office already installed on your computer, save yourself a few hundred dollars and use one of the equivalent free versions: Google Docs or Open Office. Both free versions are more than sufficient to handle even some of the more complex tasks.

Let's assume you have read the primers on spreadsheets and are familiar with some of the basic functions. We can now turn our attention to a slightly more sophisticated expense tracking approach.

Spreadsheets have a vast capacity to perform calculations of any kind but they are also very useful in presenting and analyzing data. Let's revisit our expense worksheet and find out how easy it is to record data but also how easy it is to summarize and present the data from different angles. That aspect of spreadsheets comes in very handy in our fact-finding stage when we need to analyze where most of our unnecessary spending occurs.

Once the data is in your spreadsheet, it's easy to add totals or to sort the data any way you like. Let's look at all the expenses for Food/Groceries in our mini-example again and use the free online version of Google Docs to sort and add those expense items.

With only a few transactions to enter, the spreadsheet approach might not be much more efficient than our low-tech options. But imagine having hundreds of expense items to analyze. At that point, the power of a spreadsheet application comes in very handy. With just a few clicks of a button, you can see summaries and get a complete overview of where all your money goes.

To give you a more realistic example, we can now look at a whole month's worth of data, summarize the data by categories and also show a handy chart format to illustrate where your money goes.

Suppose you gathered an entire month of expenses and entered it all into a spreadsheet (the example below only shows a partial list of sample expenses for a typical young adult).

| Date | Where My Money Went | Category | How much? |
|---|---|---|---|
| 01-Jan-11 | Dinner | Food/Groceries | 10.00 |
| 02-Jan-11 | Lunch | Food/Groceries | 3.00 |
| 03-Jan-11 | Rent | Housing | 500.00 |
| 03-Jan-11 | Lunch | Food/Groceries | 3.50 |
| 04-Jan-11 | Lunch | Food/Groceries | 3.50 |
| 05-Jan-11 | Breakfast | Food/Groceries | 3.00 |
| 05-Jan-11 | Gasoline | Transportation | 40.00 |
| 05-Jan-11 | Lunch | Food/Groceries | 4.95 |
| 05-Jan-11 | Drinks | Entertainment | 6.00 |
| 05-Jan-11 | Groceries | Food/Groceries | 30.00 |
| 05-Jan-11 | Drinks | Entertainment | 10.00 |
| 05-Jan-11 | Lunch | Food/Groceries | 4.00 |
| 06-Jan-11 | Lunch | Food/Groceries | 3.50 |
| 07-Jan-11 | Lunch | Food/Groceries | 3.00 |
| 07-Jan-11 | Dinner | Food/Groceries | 10.00 |
| 08-Jan-11 | Lunch | Food/Groceries | 5.00 |
| 08-Jan-11 | Dinner | Food/Groceries | 10.00 |
| 09-Jan-11 | Concert | Entertainment | 10.00 |
| 09-Jan-11 | Lunch | Food/Groceries | 5.50 |
| 10-Jan-11 | Lunch | Food/Groceries | 3.00 |
| 11-Jan-11 | Lunch | Food/Groceries | 2.50 |
| 12-Jan-11 | Groceries | Food/Groceries | 35.00 |
| 12-Jan-11 | Books | Education | 15.00 |
| 12-Jan-11 | Lunch | Food/Groceries | 2.50 |
| 13-Jan-11 | Lunch | Food/Groceries | 3.00 |
| 14-Jan-11 | Lunch | Food/Groceries | 2.95 |
| 14-Jan-11 | Dinner | Food/Groceries | 10.00 |
| 15-Jan-11 | Gasoline | Transportation | 40.00 |
| 15-Jan-11 | Lunch | Food/Groceries | 4.00 |
| 15-Jan-11 | Dinner | Food/Groceries | 10.00 |
| 16-Jan-11 | Concert | Entertainment | 15.00 |
| 16-Jan-11 | Lunch | Food/Groceries | 4.50 |
| 17-Jan-11 | Lunch | Food/Groceries | 2.95 |
| ... | *Additional Expenses not listed here* | | ... |

Suppose you wanted to see the totals for all categories. That's easy enough with a spreadsheet when you can sort and add subtotals with just a few clicks.

A summary of the individual categories shows the following totals:

| Category | Total |
|---|---|
| Debt/Obligations | 100.00 |
| Education | 27.00 |
| Entertainment | 41.00 |
| Food/Groceries | 361.80 |
| Housing | 675.00 |
| Miscellaneous | 3.95 |
| Personal/Health | 120.00 |
| Savings | 50.00 |
| Transportation | 120.00 |
| **Grand Total** | **1,498.75** |

Better yet, you can present your findings in a pie chart like this:

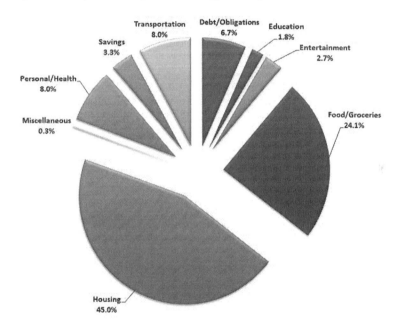

To get you started with your own expense tracking efforts, you can download this sample spreadsheet as well as a blank spreadsheet for your own personal use from our resource site (see resource section at the end of the book).

Another crucial advantage of spreadsheets is the fact that many banks, brokers and credit card companies allow you to download transactions from your account directly into Excel or you can copy them into your preferred spreadsheet application. Instead of having to gather all the receipts and manually entering data, you can save time by copying the data into your spreadsheet with just a few clicks.

As you can see, spreadsheets include powerful analytical tools and illustrations. When you have a basic understanding of spreadsheet applications, this is definitely a cool way to keep track of your personal finances.

But let's recall the main point of all these exercises: We want to track our monthly expenses to get an understanding of where our money goes. If the more complex spreadsheets work for you -- great. In case this is too complicated you can arrive at the same conclusions using the low-tech alternatives. Again, we need to find out where the money is going then embark on a strategy to reduce expenses consistently. Whichever method works for you, use it!

∽

## Personal Finance Software

Before we put on the final touches and set up our first budget, let us briefly review some of the many personal finance applications.

Personal finance software came to the forefront of consumer finances with the development of Intuit's Quicken which was an offspring of a traditional accounting application. Unlike many other traditional accounting packages, Quicken was easy to set up and extremely user-friendly even for folks without any accounting or finance background. Today, Quicken and similar programs by Intuit are still the most popular personal finance applications and they continue to evolve with ever more capabilities.

But there are many other products equally powerful that essentially do the same thing Quicken does. You are not limited to just one software provider.

Many of these systems have become so efficient and complex they tend to take over everything and almost take the mystery out of budgeting and financial planning. It's a bit like modern cars – all very efficient but nearly impossible to repair on your own because everything these days is software driven.

For instance, you can download all your online banking and credit card transactions with these systems, making your expense tracking and budgeting a lot less demanding.

You could even go one step further and sign up with Mint.com, a division of Intuit. Mint.com is the online version of Quicken. Their online service is free of charge making it very tempting to sign up.

But before you do, there are some caveats you need to consider.

Having all your financial data online and with one firm does pose a security risk no matter what this company tells you. Similar to most financial institutions, the makers of Mint.com, Quicken and other software vendors with online access promise to have the highest security measures and data encryption in place. Fair enough, they are part of a reputable organization and appear trustworthy.

Having said that, I don't feel comfortable having all of my financial information sitting somewhere on an online server, no matter how safe and secure that system promises to be. I would personally prefer to spread some of that risk among a few banks knowing quite well that it takes slightly more effort on my part to get all the data into my personal finance software.

If you're like me and have a healthy dose of built-in data paranoia, you would probably opt for an off-line solution. You can still download all of your account information from separate institutions but you can keep all your personal financial transactions in one place controlled only by you.

Other folks might take more comfort from the fact that their financial data is stored on a professional server with sophisticated backup systems. Statistically, the odds are greater that your own personal computer gets damaged, stolen or hacked into, another point speaking in favor of the online data solutions.

Again, you need to find a system that works for you and suits your lifestyle. If the low-tech version does the job, use it. If you're more of a techie and are happy with the online security protocols of firms like Mint.com, by all means use their service. No matter which method you use, keep the information updated regularly and always spot check your accounts and your expenses to see if any unusual transactions show up.

There is another point to consider. Often people buy a piece of software and think that's it. Now they can relax and not worry about their money anymore. Wrong!

Buying a piece of software doesn't make you a good saver, budgeter or financial planner. No matter what system of expense tracking, budgeting or financial planning you choose, you still have to implement your plans and be consistent with keeping a lid on your expenses. You actually have to follow the financial goals you set up.

> ### *Think About It:*
> *Software and computer systems have invaded almost every aspect of our lives – mostly for the better one should think. There is however something to be said when it comes to truly understanding a subject matter or learning a craft. The music & recording industry has undergone some tremendous changes in the past two decades, primarily driven by technology. It remains questionable though if music as an art form or craft has become better. Just because it is so inexpensive and easy to produce a record does not guarantee a higher quality of music. If anything, creativity seems to have gone amiss with the increased use of technology. That probably applies not just to music but to other creative genres and arts in general - something to think about when you consider using technology to handle all your finances.*

When it comes to keeping track of your expenses, analyzing your spending or setting up a budget, there are numerous ways to get things done. More important than the method is the consistency with which you implement your financial goals. On that note, let's start our first budget.

## Phase 3:  Get ready to budget

In terms of the budget process, we have done the first couple of steps; we tracked expenses and we examined where the money goes. Now it's time to start the actual budgeting process.

### Fixed versus Discretionary Expenses
In Phase 2, we were able to get a good overview of where our money goes. Let's look at the summary of the sample expenses one more time.

| Category | Total |
|---|---|
| Debt/Obligations | 100.00 |
| Education | 27.00 |
| Entertainment | 41.00 |
| Food/Groceries | 361.80 |
| Housing | 675.00 |
| Miscellaneous | 3.95 |
| Personal/Health | 120.00 |
| Savings | 50.00 |
| Transportation | 120.00 |
| **Grand Total** | **1,498.75** |

The major expenses were housing and the food/groceries consumed. Those two items are areas where a reduction in spending could have the most impact on our budget. Yet, some of these expenses include fixed cost. Say you were renting an apartment. It would not be so easy to lower that expense. You would either have to move or take in roommates to share the cost of the rent. Depending on your age and lifestyle, you may have other fixed expenses which are usually the more difficult ones in terms of making budget adjustments.

Discretionary spending i.e. the amount of times you go to the movies, eating out and generally all types of entertaining including shopping sprees are expenses you should consider cutting first. These also include silly expenses like late payments, overdraft charges and unnecessary high interest on credit card balances. All of those need to be eradicated completely. Remember why we learned about balancing your checkbook and checking accounts?

Prior to setting up your budget, review the categories you used for tracking your expenses in the first few weeks. You may find that some of the categories are not all that important whereas other categories might work better for you. Make those category changes now so that your budget works for you.

## Working with Subcategories

Now is also a good time to include subcategories in your budgeting process. Subcategories give you a more detailed overview of where spending occurs. You may need that level of detail to put the first spending curbs in place. For example, find out exactly how much you spend eating out versus the groceries you buy. One of the easier ways to reduce spending is simply to eat out less often. Prepare a sandwich for lunch and learn how to cook. Both can reduce your total food expenses quite a bit.

In case subcategories seem too cumbersome, just stick with your normal categories but consider expanding the category list. Using the "Food/Grocery" example again, you may want to split that up into "Eating Out" and "Groceries". Another example would be to separate housing expenses into "Rent" and "Utilities" (Gas, Water, Electricity). Again, it's important that you set up categories that work for you.

## Budget for Taxes & Insurance

As an employee, a certain amount of your paycheck is usually withheld for taxes and you are paid an amount net of taxes and other payments towards social security etc.

As an independent artist, you typically don't pay taxes each month but they eventually become due. It is extremely important that you set an appropriate amount aside for your monthly budget. Estimate your annual taxes based on the total taxes you paid during the past year plus any increase you may get if you generated more income in the current year. For instance, if you estimate to make 20% more than last year, raise your estimate for the taxes accordingly. Say you paid $3,000 in taxes in the past year and you project your income to go up by 20% this year, your estimated annual tax would be $3,600 ($3,000 + 20%).

We can now convert the estimated annual tax into our monthly budget. Simply divide $3,600 into 12 and you get $300 as a monthly budget amount towards your taxes.

Apply the same concept to other expenses that are not paid on a monthly basis. Items like car insurance and liability insurance come to mind. Don't forget to include smaller payments like annual subscriptions to magazines, certain online services and memberships. Even a $60 annual membership for an online subscription should be factored in. It's all those small expenses that can add up quickly if you aren't careful.

**Your Income**
Up to this point, we have not discussed a major component of the budget – your income. To get a good overview of your income, you should know exactly where your money is coming from. This is particularly important for anyone running his/her own business, in other words, you.

In addition, you want to know what type of job or activity generates most of your money. A musician might want to track how much money he/she can make from teaching, playing in bands or studio gigs. A composer may want to track income from film, television scores or music licensing. A graphic artist might like to find out which client and which design project produced the most income. It is also good to know which jobs or projects gave you the most headache i.e. those where you spent the most effort while getting paid very little.

> **_Think About It:_**
> Business owners across all sorts of industries tend to observe that they make most of their money from only a few clients or products. This is referred to as the **Pareto Principle** or the **80-20 Rule**. The 80-20 rule states that about 80% of the outcomes are attributed to only 20% of the causes. In plain English, many businesses derive roughly 80% of their income from only 20% of their clients or products. An artist might make 80% of his/her income from selling only a few pieces of art. In music, the extreme examples are the so-called "One-Hit-Wonders". As a working musician you might never have the fortune of creating a best-selling album but you still want to understand exactly which activity or gig generates the bulk of your income. Therefore, you should track different types of income streams within your budget. A good way to examine this analytically is to record the hours versus income generated. If you notice that 80% of your working hours are spent on certain jobs that pay very little, you may want to slowly devote more time and energy towards jobs that pay more based on the hours you spend.

When it comes to budgeting, your key to success depends on the choices and boundaries you set for your plan. Making good decisions in terms of your spending is critical to staying within your budget. Your choices in terms of generating income are equally important. In the beginning of your career you may not have the luxury of choosing between too many jobs. As you start out you have to take jobs as and when they are offered to you.

While it is important to always keep your bread and butter business, for instance a teaching gig, you should set certain boundaries and time limits on those activities generating less income. As your career progresses, you can devote more time and energy towards higher income producing jobs.

ᘒ

## Start Budgeting

To get our first budget setup, let's use some sample numbers that would apply to a young musician. Let's hook up with Chris the drummer again. Chris graduated from college and has been working for a couple of years as a professional musician. He has been working very hard and managed to get a teaching gig at a local music school. He also plays in some bands and co-writes for TV commercials with another musician. We have built our first budget around Chris' life as a working musician. Please remember that the numbers are just for illustrative purposes. Depending on where you live and what types of jobs you take on, you have to adjust the numbers accordingly so they apply to your personal circumstances.

༆

## The Short List (Income)

Your budget begins with the income component – a relatively short list for most of us who only have a few sources of income. As tough as it may seem to earn money, recording your earnings is easy. Write down the income for each of your preferred categories. In our example, let's use the following categories along with the best guess for the income generated in each category:

| Income | Budget |
|---|---|
| Teaching | 1,200.00 |
| Projects (Film/TV) | 300.00 |
| Live Performances | 400.00 |
| Recordings | 300.00 |
| Royalties | 100.00 |
| Interest/Dividends | 50.00 |
| Other | 0.00 |
| **Total Income** | **2,250.00** |

In addition to the amounts for the various jobs, we should also include an estimate of interest income from savings or other investments. The money you make by working your jobs is considered earned income. By contrast, interest income from savings and other investments is called passive or investment income.

> ### _Think About It:_
> _As you get better at handling your finances, you will notice that the amount of passive and investment income will increase in proportion to your earned income. Once you figure out how to budget and live within your means, any money that you don't spend could be used to increase your savings and to allocate more of your money towards investments and retirement planning. If you can keep improving your budget you can let more and more of your money work on your behalf. The secret to financial success is to find a good balance between earned income and passive/ investment income. As you get older, you might one day be in a position to live just from your passive income. At that point, you literally let your money work on your behalf._

# The Long List (Expenses)

Expenses are a bit harder to keep track of and also quite difficult to keep in check. The list of expenses is usually a lot longer than your income component; all the more reason to use our analytical approach in limiting our expenses to the budget plan. Let's look at some examples of expense items placed into different categories and subcategories.

## P.Y.F.

Most financial planners will tell you that an important ingredient towards a successful budget is to **pay yourself first**. Remember our essential savings goal? Our first priority was to save enough money so that we can live from the savings for an entire year. Not an easy task but that is why we put P.Y.F. on top of any other expense items. Before you pay anything else, set aside a portion of your income towards savings. Paying yourself first with consistent contributions is the fastest way to building a sizeable nest egg. In our case, Chris wants to reach his essential savings goal within four years and figured he could reach that goal by putting aside at least $200 each month and letting his money grow with the help of interest on his savings. P.Y.F. can be used in other ways to help you plan for your financial future. Until you reach your essential savings goal giving you enough of a financial safety cushion, it is best not to get distracted by any other investment or financial planning activity. Thus, our first expense category looks like this:

| Pay Yourself First | Budget |
| --- | --- |
| Checking Account | |
| *Essential Savings Goal* | *200.00* |
| Retirement | |
| Investments | |
| Other | |
| **Total Pay Yourself First** | **200.00** |

## Debt & Obligations

Chris is fortunate enough not to have any student loans or other major debt. However, he cannot ignore that taxes on earned income are due on April 15 at the very latest each year. Many independent artists, freelancer and even small business owners tend to ignore how important it is to prepare for that painful day when you have to write a big check to the U.S. Government. No matter how you look at it, taxes cannot be avoided. Consider it the cost of doing business. If you set aside an appropriate amount each month, you won't feel the pinch when taxes are due.

| Debt/Obligations | Budget |
|---|---|
| Student Loan | |
| Other Loans | |
| Credit Cards | |
| Federal Taxes | 300.00 |
| State/Local Taxes | 30.00 |
| Other | |
| **Total Debt/Obligations** | **330.00** |

### Think About It:

*Taxes and tax planning seem like a good reason to drive home the time value of money concept once more. If you can set aside a good amount of your tax payment today, let the money gain some interest in a savings account before you have to write that painful check for taxes. You won't be gaining huge sums in interest but every penny earned will effectively lower your taxes by the same amount. Knowledge of that should ease your pain a bit.*

## Education

Of all expense categories, I regard this component as one of the most critical in terms of your future career. If you are like me, you would be happy to allocate more of your disposable income towards your education. Consider any expense towards education an investment in your future and do not shy away from spending money for good quality education and educational activities.

| Education | Budget |
|---|---|
| Tuition/Lessons | |
| Books | 50.00 |
| Subscriptions | |
| Other | |
| **Total Education** | **50.00** |

In our example, we did not allocate a big amount towards education because Chris recently graduated and is now two years into his job as a musician. Education is vital in terms of getting ahead and staying competitive in your industry. But focusing on education does not necessarily mean you need to spend lots of money. Instead factor in the time you spend reading, learning and practicing your craft. All those activities are educational and you should at least allocate time, if not money, towards education.

## Entertainment

When people make their first budget they usually start their cost-cutting exercise by limiting entertainment expenses, which is absolutely fine. You pick the lowest hanging fruit first.

Having said that, if a particular type of entertainment is important to you, simply plan for it and establish a budget item. Take vacations for instance. Planning ahead gets you better deals for travel and accommodation. Also, by budgeting a small amount each month, you effectively lower the cost of the vacation (time value of money). The alternative, such as booking late or paying for a trip with a credit card, should be avoided.

Our friend Chris is certain that he will not take a vacation this year. There are too many projects lined up and he does not want to miss that all important phone call while he's surfing in Hawaii. He does, however, enjoy going to concerts and he allocates an amount each month to see a few local concerts.

| Entertainment | Budget |
|---|---|
| Concerts | 50.00 |
| Movies/Theater | 20.00 |
| Hobbies | |
| Vacation/Travel | |
| Other | |
| **Total Entertainment** | **70.00** |

### *Think About It:*

*Going to concerts, theaters and seeing movies can be entertaining but these places can also be vital for learning, networking and connecting with other like-minded people. Viewed from that angle, you may not want to completely eliminate spending for entertainment. A screenwriter could therefore allocate a higher portion of expenses towards seeing movies and theater plays. As a musician, you may consider budgeting a larger amount towards paying for concerts. As a graphic artist, designer or painter, you might earmark more dollars towards exhibitions and museum visits. Those types of expenses can also be considered educational or marketing expenses. Technically, they are part of the cost of running your business. Use your judgment to allocate these types of expenses based on your specific industry.*

## Food & Groceries

We all have to eat so there is no way to completely eliminate food and grocery expenses. But we can definitely limit unnecessary spending. Eating out at restaurants is one of those expenses that can significantly impact your budget. You could still go out to restaurants but each time you do, be more conscious of the financial impact of your menu choices. For example, many restaurants offer specials, half-size portions and coupons that can reduce your bill. Unless you are really hungry, think twice about ordering an appetizer and think even harder about ordering desert. Simply eating less makes a difference in terms of your budget. For most of us, eating less is also the healthier choice.

Many folks these days spend more money in restaurants than in grocery stores. More often than not, people's restaurant expenses are twice as much as the grocery bills. It should really be the other way around. As a guideline, your total expenses for eating out should only be about half of the money you spend on groceries. As long as you are in that ballpark, you're on the right track. Our friend Chris set his budget for Food/Groceries based on that rule of thumb.

| Food/Groceries | Budget |
|---|---|
| Groceries | 200.00 |
| Eating Out | 100.00 |
| Other | |
| **Total Food/Groceries** | **300.00** |

## Housing

The overall cost of shelter is the largest expense item for an average person. It doesn't matter whether you rent or eventually own a home, having a roof over your head doesn't come cheap. Since this is the largest expense item, we need to pay special attention to detail here.

In our example, Chris shares a three-bedroom apartment with his friend Jim. All expenses for rent, utilities etc. are shared equally among them. Since both of them are musicians they use the extra bedroom to store their instruments and equipment. For the time being, this housing solution seems to work for Chris. Chris cannot imagine moving to a location further out in the suburbs where rents are cheaper. He feels that the central location of his apartment provides easier access and faster commuting time for most of his jobs. Thus, the bulk of the housing expense category is fairly rigid and cannot be changed easily. If a central location is important for your job, having a more expensive apartment is just part of the cost of doing business.

In our example, Chris added two budget items that may seem unnecessary on first glance. However, considering that musical instruments and other expensive equipment are stored in that apartment, it is wise to insure these items. He also sets a budget of $50 towards any house related expenses. Although he rarely uses up that amount, it's a good safety cushion to have in case something needs to be replaced or repaired.

| Housing | Budget |
|---|---|
| Rent (Mortgage) | 500.00 |
| Rental (Property) Insurance | 40.00 |
| Electricity | 25.00 |
| Gas/Oil | 25.00 |
| Water/Sewer/Trash | 25.00 |
| Other | 50.00 |
| **Total Housing** | **665.00** |

> ### *Think About It:*
> *Chris is doing the right thing by giving additional allowances for unexpected situations. If all goes well, he won't need the entire budgeted amounts and he can direct more each month towards his essential savings goal. The overall cost of housing is by far his largest expense - almost one third of his budget. If for any reason circumstances change and he would see a big drop in income, he could consider taking in another roommate. Both Chris and Jim have to agree on this, of course. But they could reduce their overall cost of housing by one third. In that case, the total cost of housing would fall from $665 to $443. By giving up some of the shared space, Chris (and Jim) could save $222 each month – that's $2664 per year.*

## Miscellaneous

General expenses and anything that doesn't fit into the other categories should go towards miscellaneous expenses. Some people include expenses for telephone, Internet and TV in this category. Other folks might consider these items also part of their housing expenses. It's up to you how you group your expenses as long as you include them in your overall budget.

Chris has one additional item which is a relatively high budget amount. As a professional musician, he needs to maintain his equipment and sometimes upgrade his instruments. Obviously, he cannot afford a new drum set every six months but he might have to purchase new cymbals or percussion equipment once in a while. Setting aside an amount each month will help bring down the cost of new purchases or repairs - not by much but every penny helps. Having set aside some money for the time when you need new equipment for a specific job, you'll be able to pay for it in cash. Hasta la vista credit cards...

| Miscellaneous | Budget |
|---|---|
| Phone | 50.00 |
| Internet/TV | 25.00 |
| Equipment/Maintenance | 100.00 |
| Clubs/Memberships | 5.00 |
| Other | 40.00 |
| **Total Miscellaneous** | **220.00** |

### Personal & Health Expenses

Chris is lucky; his girlfriend is handy with scissors and he doesn't need to spend any money for haircuts. He's also not much of a dresser, hardly goes shopping for clothes and that helps him limit his personal shopping expenses.

Chris is young and in good shape. To keep it that way, Chris works out and eats well. But he also appreciates the importance of having health insurance in case something ever happens to him. When it comes to the dentist and general doctor visits, he puts aside a small amount each month. He does the same for medication and prescription drugs.

| Personal/Health | Budget |
|---|---|
| Clothing | 20.00 |
| Health Insurance | 100.00 |
| Doctor/Dentist | 40.00 |
| Medicine/Drugs | 25.00 |
| Other | |
| **Total Personal/Health** | **185.00** |

**Think About It:**

*As you get older and start having a family, the cost of health insurance increases dramatically. It is important to stay in good shape and eat healthy. Regular exercise can prevent many diseases and will eventually have a huge impact on the cost of your health insurance as well. If you are generally in good shape, you can opt for an insurance choice with higher deductibles which can bring down your monthly premium substantially. You might have to pay more out-of-pocket expenses for normal doctor visits but you can still be insured in case of major illness and hospitalization. A more recent development is the so-called "health savings account" offered by some insurers. The HSA has definite tax advantages and is somewhat similar to a retirement account.*

*The cost of staying healthy continues to increase seemingly every year, all the more reason to learn about insurance plans and possible tax advantages. Planning ahead in this scenario is vital yet again. It will help you stay in shape but also save you lots of money down the road.*

## Transportation

Last not least, here's the final expense category in our sample budget. Reliable and efficient transportation is important to get you and your equipment to your job on time. A musician living in Los Angeles simply cannot function without a car. A graphic artist living in New York on the other hand might tell you a different story. Having a car in the Big Apple really doesn't make much sense so it all depends on where you live and whether you need a lot of instruments or equipment to perform your job.

Our friend Chris lives in Los Angeles, and being a drummer, he has to have a fairly good size car to transport all his gear. Some of the expense items like insurance, gasoline and car registration are beyond his control. He can, however, do something about the overall cost of owning a car by limiting the interest cost on a car loan. Chris bought a used car when he graduated. He still has two more years of payments before the car is fully paid off. Chris' final budget category looks like this:

| Transportation | Budget |
|---|---|
| Car Payments | 100.00 |
| Car Insurance | 50.00 |
| Gasoline | 120.00 |
| Bus/Train | |
| Repairs | 50.00 |
| Registration | 30.00 |
| Other | |
| **Total Transportation** | **350.00** |

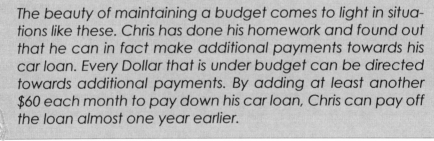

### *Think About It:*

When we examined the different types of loans we learned that there is a substantial interest burden that effectively raises the cost of anything you buy on credit. Car loans are no exception. The longer the term of the loan and the higher the interest rate, the more you end up paying for your car. In our example, Chris has two more years left to finish all payments of a four year car loan. Most consumers keep paying their monthly loan payments until the loan is fully paid up. Very few people consider making additional payments which could shorten the time and the overall cost of the loan. When you have a car loan, read the fine print and find out if the loan agreement prevents you from paying off the loan early or making additional payments. Loans with so-called prepayment penalties should be avoided.

The beauty of maintaining a budget comes to light in situations like these. Chris has done his homework and found out that he can in fact make additional payments towards his car loan. Every Dollar that is under budget can be directed towards additional payments. By adding at least another $60 each month to pay down his car loan, Chris can pay off the loan almost one year earlier.

# Budget Summary

When you are done with the individual budget categories, it's time to summarize and to get a complete overview of the entire budget. If it's done correctly, the budget balances income and expenses. Our summary looks like this:

| Income | Budget |
|---|---|
| Teaching | 1,200.00 |
| Projects (Film/TV) | 300.00 |
| Live Performances | 400.00 |
| Recordings | 300.00 |
| Royalties | 100.00 |
| Interest/Dividends | 50.00 |
| Other | |
| **Total Income** | **2,350.00** |

| Expenses | Budget |
|---|---|
| P.Y.F. | 200.00 |
| Debt | 330.00 |
| Education | 50.00 |
| Entertain | 70.00 |
| Food | 300.00 |
| Housing | 665.00 |
| Misc. | 200.00 |
| Pers./Health | 185.00 |
| Transport | 350.00 |
| **Total Expenses** | **2,350.00** |

| **Net Overall** | **0.00** |
|---|---|

***Think About It:***
*Next time you read the newspaper and learn that some politicians are calling for a "balanced budget" or "balanced budget amendment", you can see now why it is so important to balance the budget. It might also be a bit clearer now how most governments fail miserably in that task.*

# Implementing Your Budget

At the beginning of this chapter, I mentioned that the key to getting financially ahead was to establish AND keep realistic budgets. Our first budget looks pretty good on paper. How well can we actually keep up with this plan? To set our plan in motion let's add some more functionality to the budget.

Just as we did in our fact finding stage, we need to keep tracking our budget items and compare actual numbers with our planned targets. The best way to do this is to put both side by side. Here is an example of how Chris' budget compares to actual figures having tracked all items for one month.

| Income | Budget | Actual | Difference |
|---|---|---|---|
| Teaching | 1,200.00 | 1,200.00 | |
| Projects (Film/TV) | 300.00 | 250.00 | -50.00 |
| Live Performances | 400.00 | 400.00 | |
| Recordings | 300.00 | 300.00 | |
| Royalties | 100.00 | 100.00 | |
| Interest/Dividends | 50.00 | 20.00 | -30.00 |
| Other | | | |
| **Total Income** | **2,350.00** | **2,270.00** | **-80.00** |

| Expenses | Budget | Actual | Difference |
|---|---|---|---|
| P.Y.F. | 200.00 | 250.00 | 50.00 |
| Debt/Obligations | 330.00 | 330.00 | |
| Education | 50.00 | 30.00 | -20.00 |
| Entertainment | 70.00 | 70.00 | |
| Food/Groceries | 300.00 | 325.00 | 25.00 |
| Housing | 665.00 | 635.00 | -30.00 |
| Misc. | 200.00 | 165.00 | -35.00 |
| Personal/Health | 185.00 | 120.00 | -65.00 |
| Transportation | 350.00 | 285.00 | -65.00 |
| **Total Expenses** | **2,350.00** | **2,210.00** | **-140.00** |
| **Net Overall** | **-** | **60.00** | **60.00** |

This first budget seems to work so far. Although the income was slightly lower than projected, Chris was able to make up for the shortfall by trimming down a few other expenses. Overall, he is $60 ahead in his budget. He could use the extra $60 towards paying down more on his car loan as we discussed earlier.

Keep in mind that your financial circumstances can change suddenly. This is particularly important for self-employed musicians and artists with highly fluctuating income. Therefore, you cannot simply establish a budget and stick to it blindly. Budget adjustments need to be made when financial circumstances change. When your income declines in one month, recognize it early and tighten your spending belt in some other areas. As much as possible, you want your net income to stay positive each month. I find it much easier to make small adjustments early rather than trying to catch up later on. That is one reason why you should not concern yourself too much with a yearly budget for now. Keep focusing on your monthly budget and as soon as you project a decline in income, adjust your expenses to reflect those changes.

## Tips To Stay Within Budget

### Stay On Top
Record your expenses regularly and often. When we first started tracking our expenses, I recommended keeping a spending diary. Make it a habit and continue updating your expenses every day. Just like brushing your teeth, it should only take a couple of minutes. Spreadsheets or personal finance software can make your budgeting and planning easier. But more important than the tool you use to track your spending is a consistent approach to budgeting. Once you have developed a habit, the payoff can be huge. Staying on top off your expenses allows you to live within your means.

### Analyze Your Spending Habits
Writing down your expenses is already half the ticket towards greater prosperity. The most obvious spending sins stand out the most. It's also a good idea to do a brief weekly review of the major expenses you had during the week. That's a good time to compare how you are doing in terms of your budget limits. If your monthly budget for eating out is $100 and you had just spent $60 in the first week, you know that you have to step on the brakes to stay within budget in the remaining three weeks.

### Balance Your Checkbook
Review your bank account(s) and balance your check book at least once a month. Even though you have a budget, you still have to monitor your accounts and make sure that there are no errors. Small mistakes can easily lead to bounced checks or overdrafts. Avoid silly fees by verifying that your accounts are always in good standing.

### Build Flexibility Into Your Budget
The incomes of freelancers, artists and musicians can fluctuate quite a bit. Be flexible in your budget approach and adjust your expenses as much as you can when you see a big change in income during one month.

Another way to build flexibility into your budget is to give it extra padding for unforeseen expenses. You may have noticed that each of our budget categories had one subcategory called "Other". That is an ideal way to budget a small amount for all those unforeseen expenses that usually come your way. Again, use your budget amounts as guidelines but do make adjustments when circumstances change.

# More Money Saving Tips

When it comes to handling your finances, common sense is probably the best approach to get financially ahead. These days, there are lots of useful websites that give additional tips to help you with your personal finances. Some sites focus on credit and debt, others on investments. But there is also more help available for a basic common sense approach to living within your means – the frugal living websites come to mind. Here are some additional ideas to help you save more money.

### Need Versus Want

The temptation of sale items can be big. We get bombarded by special deals, extra savings, discounts, coupons and a host of other spending incentives on a daily basis. The world of advertising has done a remarkable achievement. Over the years, they have framed the word savings into something that has nothing to do with saving but everything to do with spending money. Perfect time to dispel some myths here:

First off, the word "savings" is a complete misnomer in the context of advertising. The only way for you to "save money" is not to spend it. Your money in a savings account, money market account or a CD – that is saving. When you go shopping, you may pay a lower price on a sale item, **but you are definitely not saving**.

Second, prices always change buying behavior; there's simply no way around it. But instead of giving in to impulses, ask yourself this: Would you still buy that gadget if it wasn't on sale? If the answer is yes, then you might have a more legitimate reason that this gadget is something you really need.

If the answer is no, go back home and practice your instrument, create a new song or a piece of artwork. That will not only save you some money but it may create some future revenues for you.

### Eliminate Bad Habits

Eat less, drink less and eliminate the so-called bad habits. It can save you loads of money. Instead, exercise often and live healthier. It's all part of the concept of living within your means.

### Use Cash More Often

There's something about spending real dollar bills instead of using plastic money. Most people feel the pinch a lot more when they hand over cash rather than a credit card. Using cash tends to inhibit your spending.

Using cash or debit cards can also make a difference for some purchases. Credit card companies charge their vendors somewhere between 2-3%

for each purchase customers make with their credit cards. Most gas stations these days add that 2% charge to the price of gasoline – check it next time you fill up your car. Retail stores are not quite there yet but talk to vendors to see if they can give you a discount for a cash purchase.

**Buy A Rice Cooker**
Invest $30-$40 in an electric rice cooker which is a very versatile piece of cooking equipment. It can cook, steam and reheat just about anything in addition to cooking rice. It can also help you save lots of money down the road. Yes you might need to learn how to cook a little but that skill can be a tremendous cost cutting tool as well. You simply eat more at home.

There are many more tips for saving money and frugal living. Spend a bit of time thinking about your lifestyle and you can come up with at least another handful of good money saving habits.

# SEVEN

## *The Far Out Stuff*

We have come so far in this book and discovered all these amazing things about money. By now, your financial literacy skills should be well beyond the beginner's level. That said, a book about money would not be complete without at least touching on some of the basics of financial markets and investing. We won't be able to learn all there is to know about investing in just one chapter - hundreds of books have been devoted to the subject. But you will get a good overview of financial markets, get introduced to some of the vocabulary and learn how to avoid some of the biggest pitfalls when it comes to investing. Finally, we will round things up with some book recommendations.

### Economics in 5 Minutes

Presumably you took an economics class in High School or you may have taken an Econ 101 class in college. Economics can get a bit dull but the principles of economics are as fascinating as people themselves. Unlike Math, Physics or other hard sciences, economic equations don't seem to add up as accurately as the formulas might suggest. No wonder Economics is also called the "dismal science".

Basic economic principles can be narrowed down to one predominant conundrum: *Scarcity*.

As a whole, society has unlimited wants but very limited resources. At the time of this writing, the world population is about 6.8 billion people - all competing for the same limited resources. Economists try to make sense of this conundrum, not just in terms of financial aspects but also with regard to the wider implications for society.

The dismal science can be as controversial as it is complex. Our excursion into the dismal science shall therefore remain short and sweet.

ᔆ

## Supply and Demand

In the more or less free market society that we live in, the price of nearly everything is determined by supply and demand. This does not only affect financial markets but all kinds of goods and services.

Here's a hypothetical scenario to explain supply and demand...

*If you were the only drummer in town who can play a tango and tango fever suddenly hit the city, a few things would happen:*

*Everyone would want to hear you play, your telephone would ring off the hook and you might have to work several gigs each day. Say the tango fever persists, after a few days you might have people offering you more money to play the tango for them. The next call comes in and you would be compelled to raise your hourly rate. Still more people want to hear you play the tango. You continue to raise your rates until your phone rings a bit less. People now start thinking twice as to whether they want to spend $500 an hour to hear you play.*

*As the tango fever persists, word spreads around and a tango drummer who lives in another city hears of the prices people are willing to pay just to hear you play the tango. This drummer packs his bags and drives to your town. Now there are two drummers who can play the tango both charging very high prices for their tango performance. Before you know it, two more drummers move to your city and all four can play the same tango and make a living. But now, your phone only rings a few times each week and you are not nearly as busy as before. The other drummers also realize that they sit around waiting for calls more and more. One drummer has an idea. He starts to advertise his tango skills but charges only $250 an hour. Word of this cheap tango performer spreads and more people start calling him for gigs. The other three drummers notice that their phones slowly stop ringing. Eventually, they find out what happened and are forced to lower their prices as well. All tango drummers continue to lower their prices until each of them has enough work making less money per hour but can still make a living as long as tango fever in this town persists.*

*Can you see how the supply and demand for a specific skill – drumming a tango – can affect the price? Let's remember this basic economic principle as we start learning about investments.*

ᗡ

## Introduction To Investing & Financial Markets

Before we delve into the world of financial markets, here's a reminder from Chapter Five:

Don't dabble in the markets until you reach your essential savings goal!

With that in mind let's examine the main types of investments and asset classes.

## Stocks & Stock Markets

Stocks or shares are ownership parts in a company. When you buy stocks you are a part owner of a company. There are two main reasons why people like to invest in stocks:

A) <u>Price Appreciation</u>

When a company is successful and its products are popular, more people want to buy stock in that company hoping to take part of its economic success. As a result, the share price of that company increases (remember our tango lesson on supply and demand?). As share prices increase, anyone who bought the stock prior to the increase feels wealthier. At some point investors may cash in some of their gains by selling their shares at a higher price.

<u>Example</u>

Just after the big market crash in 2008, Stella bought 50 shares of Apple computers at $100. In December 2010, Apple shares were trading at about $300. She was considering whether to cash in some profits by selling her shares. Here are the numbers:

Buy 50 shares @ $100 =     $5,000 *(Cost of purchase a.k.a. cost basis)*
Sell 50 shares @ $300 =    <u>$15,000</u> *(Proceeds from sale)*
**Profit:**                **$10,000**

If Stella were to sell all of her 50 shares at $300, she could book an amazing profit of $10,000.

B) <u>Dividends</u>

Some companies distribute part of their profits in the form of so-called dividends. As a stock holder or part owner in that company, you are entitled to a fractional share of the profits of the company. When dividends are declared, every stockholder receives a certain Dollar (or penny) amount for each share he or she owns.

Not all companies distribute part of their profits. Hi-tech firms and so-called growth companies choose to re-invest all their profits towards R&D (research & development) or to fund their expansion plans. Apple is one of those firms that constantly re-invests its profits to come up with new products. But there are many companies that regularly issue dividends. Utility companies and big industrial firms tend to issue dividends more frequently. There are also companies who are somewhere in between. IBM is an example of a high-tech company that issues dividends quite often.

## Example

Let's assume Stella bought IBM shares instead of Apple around the same time. She could have bought IBM stock at about $90 per share. In December 2010 IBM was trading around $145. If Stella were to sell her shares in the market, she could make a profit of $55 per share ($145 selling price minus $90 buying price). Instead Stella decides to hang on to her shares. In the meantime however, Stella did get some additional benefits in the form of dividends. IBM currently issues a dividend of $2.60 per share each year. Dividends are usually issued every quarter and in this case, Stella would receive $0.65 per share every three months as long as she owns IBM shares and granted IBM continues to issue dividends.

If Stella had owned IBM for 2 years, she would receive a total of:

**$2.60 x 2 (years) x 50 shares = $260 in dividends.**

### Growth versus Dividends

These two examples show the brighter side of investing in stocks. But what is better for you, investing in growth stocks or dividend stocks?

As you may have heard, investing in stocks does not come without risk. On average, growth stocks tend to be more risky than companies who are more established and pay higher dividends. A good counter example for Apple would be Yahoo. If you had bought Yahoo stocks at the top of the dotcom era at about $100 per share you would not be as happy as the company name might suggest. In the 10 years since then, Yahoo's share price never reached its peak again and at the end of 2010 it was trading at just over $16 per share. Ever since Yahoo went public, it never issued a single dividend either.

By contrast, examine a typical dividend company like General Electric. Say you bought GE stocks in 2000 at $50 and held on to it. At the end of 2010, GE was trading at about $18. Although the loss would still be substantial, it is not quite as bad as that of Yahoo. Better yet, in all the years, General Electric issued dividends from their profits. Over the 10-year period, GE issued almost $9 in dividends per share. When you add dividends to the overall investment return, companies like GE are somewhat less risky than the average growth stock paying no dividends at all. When viewed from the company's perspective, a big industrial company or utility firm often has to pay higher dividends to attract investors. If the company's growth potential is not as attractive as a hot item company like Apple, a higher dividend is needed to entice investors to buy the stock.

### No Pain, No Gain

As you can see from our examples, investing in stocks can be risky. Why do we still invest in stocks then?

When people invest in stocks, they want something in return for handing over their money. By investing in stocks, they have a chance (although by no means a guarantee) to earn higher rewards than just keeping their money in a savings account. For that chance to earn higher returns, investors are willing to take on a bigger risk as well. This so-called risk-reward relationship is prevalent throughout all financial markets. Investors want higher returns for accepting bigger risks and vice versa. We will discuss risk and risk management in more detail later in this chapter.

∽

## The (In)Famous Stock Market

As companies get bigger they can raise additional capital by issuing shares to the public through a listing on a stock exchange. When a company issues new shares, they sell their shares through an Initial Public Offering (IPO). IPO's became famous during the dotcom era of the 1990s when investors of all kinds lined up to get their hands on newly issued shares. Shares from IPOs are first sold at a fixed price prior to trading on the stock exchange. But they are not easily available and get allotted through investment banks who underwrite the IPO. Unless you have a substantial account with an investment bank or a broker, it is very hard to get your hands on newly issued shares.

You can however, buy those shares when they are first publicly traded on the stock exchange. Subsequently these shares are then bought and sold many times, changing owners over and over. In the 1990s many internet stocks had massive price increases in just the first day of trading, giving the holders of IPO shares an instant gain. That is why IPO's were so popular; many investors wanted to take advantage of this golden opportunity to make some quick profits. As we all now know, the dotcom bubble burst and most of the Internet stocks that promised these illusive returns have vanished and are now but a distant memory.

***Think About It:***
*Often overlooked is the fact that companies issue shares to raise capital. In essence, they are asking for a loan from investors like you and me. Viewed from that perspective, shouldn't we do our homework and learn everything there is to know about the company that is using our money?*

### How to Buy Shares
Stocks are traded on stock exchanges. In the old days, exchanges were places were traders gathered to buy and sell shares on the trading floor

of the exchange. You can probably imagine how those traders had to scream and use hand gestures to negotiate stock prices. At times, markets went wild and the action on the trading floor was not much different from a major sporting event - just as noisy but also physically and emotionally challenging when prices were on the move.

The New York Stock Exchange (NYSE) is the most well-known stock exchange situated at the famous location of 11 Wall Street in New York City. NYSE is one of the oldest exchanges in the world and some trading is still handled by the traders on the trading floor of the exchange. The majority of all transactions these days are handled electronically though. NASDAQ, for instance, is a purely electronic market place. All transactions on NASDAQ are executed through electronic trading systems only.

Investors who want to buy shares must do so via a broker. You need to open an account with a broker and deposit some money before you can do your stock trades. Although most brokers still allow you to place trades over the phone, the majority of all transactions these days are done online. Investors can access their brokerage accounts via the internet just like online banking. Brokerage firms give their clients online access to research, account information and a myriad of sophisticated trading tools. Buying and selling shares today is as easy as clicking a few buttons.

### About Stock Indexes
You hear and read about the stock market in the daily news flashes. But what are these stock indexes exactly and what does it mean when the Dow was up by 100 points?

The Dow Jones Industrial Average a.k.a. the Dow is one of the oldest stock indexes and it tracks the performance of 30 large companies.

Another index is the Standard & Poor's 500 better known as the S&P 500 Index. This index tracks 500 of the largest companies in the U.S. Because of its broad selection of companies from all industries, it is widely considered the benchmark for US stock market performance.

Yet another index is the NASDAQ composite which tracks primarily growth and technology stocks. This index became popular during the dotcom era when many new Internet stocks were listed on the NASDAQ stock exchange and were then included in the index.

There are many more indexes but these three are the most closely watched market indexes at the moment. The way the index values are tracked and calculated differs but they use some form of weighted averages for price performance or market value of the companies that are included in the index. Although the Dow is one of the oldest and most widely talked about stock index, the finance industry uses the S&P 500 as a benchmark for the U.S. stock market performance.

৩

# Brief Introduction to Bonds

Not nearly as exciting and perhaps a bit more mysterious than stocks are investments in bonds. Bonds are called debt securities. That means a bond is a piece of paper stating who owes money to whom and under what terms - much like an ordinary I.O.U.

Bonds are issued to finance all sorts of projects and activities. Governments and municipalities issue bonds to finance big public construction projects or to pay for general government overhead. Corporations issue bonds to finance their operations and to pay for large capital expenditures such as major machinery.

Investors buy bonds and lend their money to the government or to corporations for a specified period of time - anywhere from 3 months to 30 years. In return for getting your money, the bond issuers promise a fixed dollar amount as interest payment. This fixed amount is also called the coupon rate and it is usually paid every six months. Because coupon rates are fixed, Bonds are also referred to as fixed-income securities.

To keep this bond primer short and sweet we will focus on Government Bonds from hereon. U.S. Government Bonds are referred to as Treasury Securities and they are further distinguished as Treasury bills, notes and bonds. Most investors call them T-bills, T-notes and T-bonds but for our purposes, let's just call them Treasuries.

You can buy Treasuries through your broker or directly from the government via www.treasurydirect.com.
Treasuries have different time lengths called maturities. T-bills have the shortest maturity (less than one year) whereas T-bonds can last up to 30 years. T-notes are the most widely traded Treasuries with a maturity of up to 10 years.

Having learned about the time value of money, you can imagine that the different maturities also result in different interest rates. Generally speaking, the longer the maturity the higher the interest rate. That should make sense to us now. In exchange for lending your money for a longer period of time, you want to be compensated with higher interest rates.

## The Biggest Misconception About Bonds

Treasuries are first issued at government auctions. They are then traded in the bond market just like stocks are traded in the stock market. The fact that bonds are traded can have a profound impact on your investment returns. To understand why, we need to learn about a fundamental relationship between interest rates and the prices of bonds.

In theory, Treasuries are rock-solid investments because of the government guarantee that comes along with it. That guarantee refers to the principal, the total amount of bonds you originally bought, being paid back to you at maturity. The face value or par value of a bond is set at 100 when first issued. The full amount or face value will be repaid to the bond holder at maturity.

Most long-term bond investors though do not keep their bonds for the entire time.

As a result of trading, bond prices tend to fluctuate and they have an inverse relationship with interest rates. When interest rates rise, bond prices fall and vice versa.  This is how it looks like:

**Bond Prices**

**Interest Rates**

Let's do an example to show you how a rise in interest rates could affect your bond investment.

Meet Joanne, a film editor doing freelance work for MTV. Joanne has been saving up money for the past few years and feels that she is now ready to invest some of her money. She is terrified by the possibility of losing even a little of her hard earned money. Some of her friends recommend that she should invest in Treasuries because they are guaranteed by the U.S. government and therefore "risk-free."

Joanne opens an account with a broker and buys 10 T-notes @ $1,000 each for a total of $10,000. These T-notes pay a coupon rate of 5% each year so Joanne should receive a check of $250 every six months for as long as she holds this bond. After ten years then, Joanne is guaranteed to receive back the principal, her initial $10,000 investment. Everything goes as planned and she is receiving a check of $250 every six months.

After three years, Joanne needs some cash for a down payment on a new car. She knows she can sell her T-notes back to the market and calls
168

her broker to do the transaction. Unfortunately, in the past six months, interest rates went up by 2% due to higher inflation. Other bond investors therefore would not want to buy Joanne's T-notes for $1,000 face value when they can get new T-notes that pay a coupon of 7%. As a result, the current market price for Joanne's T-notes falls to $950 for each bond. If Joanne was to sell her entire bond investment, she would only receive $9,500 at the current market prices. If interest rates were to stay at 7% or rise even higher, Joanne would have to wait another seven years until her T-notes mature and only then could she get back her principal in full.

### Think About It:

Joanne invests her $10,000 in 10-year T-notes which are considered rock solid investments because they are guaranteed by the US government. However, the guarantee for her Treasuries only extends to the coupon payments of $50 per year (5% for each $1,000 Bond) and that the principal will be paid back in full at maturity. An investor who needs his money back before maturity is exposed to interest rate risk. Longer dated Bonds have a much higher interest rate risk than short dated bonds. Therefore you still have to be careful and evaluate your long-term investments. Despite the government guarantee, you could still end up losing some money if bond prices were to fall in response to higher interest rates. If you are considering an investment in bonds, remember that bond prices and interest rates are inversely related. Only consider a longer-term bond investment with funds that you won't need to access in the short term.

The story doesn't end here, though. If interest rates were to fall from 5% to say 3%, Joanne's T-notes would now be more sought after by other investors. In that case, she could sell her bonds above face value. The market price of 10-year T-notes may have gone up to say $1,100 per bond. In addition to the coupon payments, Joanne could then also book a gain from selling her T-bonds in the market.

This example emphasizes the risk-reward relationship of investments again. The greater the risk, the higher the potential reward and vice versa. If you don't want to take any financial risk, cash and cash equivalents like savings accounts are probably your best investment options. But don't expect any great returns from those. No pain, no gain!

Stocks, bonds and cash (or cash equivalents like savings) form the three major asset classes of financial investments.

Property is also an asset class on its own but it is usually not included in financial assets. In theory, you could invest in any type of physical asset like furniture, cars, stamps, or jewelry. Although eBay has made it a lot easier to buy and sell almost anything, these types of assets cannot easily be bought and sold in just a few minutes and are therefore not considered liquid assets. Because these assets are quite unique, it is often harder to establish a price or to find a buyer.

Property is considered the most illiquid asset. This is particularly evident when house prices are declining. Some property owners have to wait for a year or even longer to get their house sold when the demand for housing dries up.

⌀

## What To Buy & When To Buy

Stocks, bonds and cash are the three major financial asset classes that average investors typically invest in. In modern finance, the concepts of asset allocation and diversification play an important role which is based on the old saying:

### *Don't put all your eggs in one basket.*

In practice, this means that you want to spread your investments among different asset classes (asset allocation) and also diversify within each asset class (diversification). As an average investor, it is difficult to figure out which stock or which bond to buy and equally difficult to figure out when to buy and when to sell.

Timing is everything, not just in music but also when it comes to investing. Almost all companies have their moments of glory and periods of setbacks. Stock prices reflect the financial success of a company to a large extent. Therefore, an investor could become wealthy by identifying the exact moment when a company becomes successful and investing in shares of that company. Whom to buy and when to buy is of course the multi-million dollar question.

Stock pickers believe they can outperform other investors by selecting only the "good" companies. Going one step further, some of the stock pickers time their buy and sell orders hoping to gain some additional advantage trading in and out of the markets. The most audacious bunch of those stock pickers are the so-called day-traders who often buy and sell the same shares within a day just trying to take small advantages from stock price movements. Statistical research will tell you however, that most day-traders are doing rather poorly and typically burn most of their money within a few years if not sooner.

The same research will also tell you that buying just a handful of stocks does not provide a good diversification and is therefore considered poor financial risk management. But most average investors do not have enough money to buy, say, 50 or more stocks to properly spread the risk. This dilemma led to the popularity of mutual funds. Mutual funds gave even the small investors an ability to spread their investment risk among the entire market.

∽

## About Mutual Funds

Mutual funds are setup as investment companies that allow investors to pool their money to invest in a selection of stocks and/or bonds. The funds are then managed by professional money managers who try to maximize gains from those investments.

Overall, mutual funds have been a good development for individual investors who would otherwise have a difficult time investing in a broader selection of stocks. Most investors also don't have the time or the knowledge to assess what stocks to buy and therefore leave the investment selection to professional managers.

### Surprise, Surprise...

You might be surprised to learn that the vast majority of mutual funds DO NOT outperform the overall market index. Depending on the sources of research and the time frame observed, about 70%-80% of mutual funds are not performing better than the benchmark index S&P 500. The rationale for this surprising phenomenon can be narrowed down to the following:

a) In a sector with thousands of mutual fund companies, there have to be some winners and losers. By definition, the average performer should be pretty much the same as the overall market.

b) Transaction costs from trading, commissions and management fees for mutual fund managers are paid from the total of all invested funds. Mutual funds charge at least 1% in fees each year. Over time, this makes it harder for each fund to keep up with or outperform the market index.

∽

## The Best Options For Average Investors

If individual stocks are too risky and mutual funds too expensive, what else can an average investor do, you might ask?

For starters, you should never put all your eggs in one basket but we'll get to that in more detail shortly. Instead of trying to pick just a few individual stocks, you should invest in a low cost index tracking fund. A few mutual funds, for instance some of the Vanguard Group of funds, offer index tracking funds with very low annual fees. The rationale here is simple. Rather than trying to outperform the market, just match the market performance and you should be better off than about 75% of all investors owning traditional mutual funds with high fees.

A more recent development in the financial industry have been so-called Exchange Traded Funds (ETFs) which are set to track an index rather than selecting only some stocks in the market. There are ETFs for the major indexes such as the Dow, S&P 500, NASDAQ and many more. The main advantage of these ETFs is the low cost to the investor. A typical mutual fund charges 1% or more in management fees. The best ETFs however, charge only about 0.1% in fees.

---

### *Think About It:*

*Most brokers and even some financial advisors tend to recommend traditional Mutual Funds over Index Tracking Funds. Their argument is that a mutual fund can pick the best stocks out of several thousand stocks in the entire market. By selecting only winners, their performance should be better than the market. However, the real reason why brokers recommend Mutual Funds is the fact that they get paid a commission to do so. As luck would have it, brokers do need to eat too. Given a choice between two seemingly equal investment options, they would of course be inclined to recommend the investment paying them the highest commission.*

*Moreover, as logic will tell you, not everybody can be above average. In reality, about 75% of mutual fund managers are not out-performing the market if you factor in all the fees. That still leaves you with, say, 25% of mutual funds who are extremely good performers. If you can get your hands on the best ones, you might be one step ahead of the rest. But that still leaves you with the same dilemma, picking stocks or picking fund managers? How do you know which ones will be the winners in the future?*

---

## Derivatives – The WMD's of Finance

*"Derivatives are financial weapons of mass destruction"*
*– Warren Buffett, legendary investor & philanthropist.*

Below are a few more details on derivatives, mainly to tell you: **Stay away from them!**

Derivatives are complex financial products where pricing is "derived" from an underlying asset. I like to think of derivatives as financial bets on a price or an event in the future. For example, an option that the share price of Coca Cola would reach $75 in six months would be a derivative.

Futures and Options are the most well-known derivatives. But the financial crisis of 2008/2009 also brought to light some other financial instruments with elegant names like "Collateralized Debt Obligations" (CDO's), "Collateralized Mortgage Obligations" (CMO's) or "Credit Default Swaps" (CDS).

While Futures and Options typically derive their pricing from a single asset e.g. Crude Oil, the fancier ones derive their pricing from more than one, often an entire basket of assets. The most complex of these financial products are derived using quantitative financial models, packaged as Structured Products and are then sold to sophisticated investors and financial institutions.

Although this all sounds fancy, rest assured that these are all highly risky types of investments. The only thing you have to remember about derivatives is to stay away from them. Take it from someone who has been involved in derivatives trading for almost two decades. Unless you have a thorough understanding of financial markets, above average discipline and substantial capital, DO NOT trade derivatives. As the financial crisis of 2008/2009 re-emphasized, even the most sophisticated institutions that should have the understanding and financial resources to assess the inherent risks of these derivatives were not able to handle them.

> ### Think About It:
> *For lack of a better word, derivatives are essentially bets on a future financial outcome. As with all bets on uncertain outcomes, the odds are typically against you. Even in a straightforward financial bet like a futures contract, the odds of making money on a trade are at best 50/50 minus transaction costs – very similar to the odds in Las Vegas actually.*

৩০

## Leverage: A Double-Edged Sword

Something that unites all derivatives is the huge leverage investors take on when trading these financial instruments. In essence, investors borrow money – a lot of money - to take on a financial bet. As an example, the leverage on a futures contract can be as high as 100:1. That means a futures trader would only come up with $1 of his own money but borrow the remaining $99 to trade a futures contract. Leverage works in your favor amplifying your profits when you make the right trading decisions. However, when you put on a bad trade and the market goes against you, it also multiplies your losses. Leverage is the main reason why over 80% of traders using derivatives end up losing money over time.

---

### *Think About It:*

*During the first decade of the 21st century the U.S. experienced a housing boom of unparalleled proportions. Within just a few years, some home-owners saw their house prices double and at some point everyone wanted to take part of this boom to reap financial gains. The housing boom eventually turned into a bubble that burst around 2006/2007. Many home-owners got wiped out, no longer being able to afford their mortgages or owing more to the banks than their house was worth. How could that have happened?*

*Aside from the many other contributing factors, including fraudulent lending practices, there was one main culprit. The root of the U.S. housing problem can be found in the extreme leverage home buyers took on when financing their home purchases. Think about this comparison for a moment:*

*In some extreme cases, home-buyers were able to finance their home loans without a down payment. These so-called "zero-down" mortgages were pushed by very aggressive lenders towards the end of the housing bubble. Little did people realize that no money down mortgages were actually more risky than trading derivatives. Here's why:*

*When sophisticated investors trade derivatives, they also take on huge leverage at the most extreme 100:1 on certain financial futures contracts. Gold futures for instance have a leverage of about 20:1 which is equivalent to a 5% down payment for a home loan. By now, we should know how risky futures are and realize that a small loss could be amplified through the extreme leverage. The unsuspecting home buyer however, who bought a house with no money down had essentially unlimited leverage - much more than Gold futures and even more than the most highly leveraged futures contracts allowed by law. Are you with me in wondering why on earth "zero-down" mortgages could have ever been allowed to be sold to the public?*

# Your Financial Plan

We finally arrived at the heart of our endeavor to make some sense of the confusing world of money and finance. After reading this book so far, you're probably still a bit unsure as to how you should manage your financial life. No worries, we have covered so much information, it takes some time for all of this to sink in. You can always go back and reread those sections that aren't so clear yet. The second time through, you should have a decent understanding of how all of this fits together.

The good news is that putting on the final touches in the form of a simple financial plan is actually not that hard anymore. As a general rule, budgeting and financial planning should be kept simple. Complicated plans do not produce better results. Keeping it simple is an approach that works in art, music, business as well as in finance. Once you find the right balance that works for you, just keep on doing it over and over again.

That said, let's put together a real simple financial plan to help you with your career and financial future.

### First Steps

Remember from the previous chapters that the key to financial success is the concept of living within your means. One key component to making this concept work for you is to setup a realistic budget and follow the budget as much as you can. We also learned that it is very important to "pay yourself first" as it helps you accelerate the contributions towards your essential savings goal.

Most financial planners will tell you to have a safety cushion of about 3-6 months in savings. But my personal rule is to have at least one year's worth of living expenses saved up. As we concluded, anyone who is self-employed needs a bigger safety cushion to deal with periods when income may dry up between projects. Our essential savings goal therefore is higher than financial planners would normally recommend.

We also used the essential savings goal as a threshold before considering any type of investing. Having covered the basics about Stocks and Bonds we must now learn how to put together an investment portfolio that is easy to implement while still trying to maximize your investment returns.

೧೨

# A Simple Investment Portfolio

Many studies have been conducted about the profitability of investing in stocks and bonds. Over a longer period of time, say, 15, 20 years or more, stocks tend to outperform bond investments by a considerable margin.

However, in the short term and anywhere from 1-10 years, historic returns on stocks have seen wild fluctuations whereas bonds provide more steady returns on average. Your investment horizon is therefore a critical component of setting up a financial plan.

Most financial experts will tell you that a sensible asset allocation and diversification is the best approach to building a successful investment portfolio.

By combining asset classes that are showing different price movements you can reduce risk and produce steadier returns. Having a mix of bonds, stocks and cash in your portfolio is the first important aspect of building your portfolio. Diversification of different investments in each asset class further reduces risk and improves returns.

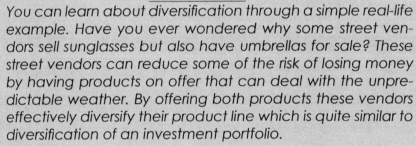

### Think About It:

*You can learn about diversification through a simple real-life example. Have you ever wondered why some street vendors sell sunglasses but also have umbrellas for sale? These street vendors can reduce some of the risk of losing money by having products on offer that can deal with the unpredictable weather. By offering both products these vendors effectively diversify their product line which is quite similar to diversification of an investment portfolio.*

For an almost simplistic but extremely powerful approach to asset allocation, I'd like to refer to a concept called an **age-based asset allocation**. This concept was made popular by John Bogle, the founder of the Vanguard Group of Funds. John Bogle suggests using your age as a guideline for the percentage of bonds in your portfolio. If you were 50 years old, 50% of your investment assets should be in bonds. If you were 25, only 25% of your assets should be in bonds, the remaining 75% in stocks.

The rationale for John Bogle's approach is quite simple:

When you are young, your investment horizon (typically the number of years until your retirement) is of course much longer than say someone at age 60. Stocks have historically outperformed bonds but they can be quite volatile within a shorter time span, say up to 10 years. When you are 25 and you have about 40 years until retirement, you should not be too concerned about short-term market corrections as the market tends to reverse and make up for losses in the long-term. If you had most of your assets invested in cash or bonds only, you could lose out on the much higher profit potential from owning stocks.

In short, a good balance between stocks, bonds and cash are the best way to start.

Let's assume you are 25 now and you have about $10,000 to invest after having fulfilled your essential savings goal.

Based on John Bogle's approach, you could invest $2,500 in bonds and $7,500 in stocks, giving you an asset allocation of 25% bonds and 75% stocks. Among these two asset classes, you should also diversify to further reduce risk and enhance returns.

**Diversifying your Bond Allocation**
John Bogle is a passionate supporter of bonds but let's remember that bonds are not without risk unless you hold them until maturity. You can further diversify some of that risk by investing in low-cost bond funds or bond ETFs who typically invest in many different kinds of bonds with varying maturities, again to spread some risk. For instance, you could select a diversified bond fund to take care of the needed diversification and you'd be set.

If you don't like the idea of having some small risk in your bond component of the portfolio, you could replace the bond allocation with a similar allocation of CDs (Certificates of Deposits). CDs are a good alternative to bonds in that they guarantee the principal as well.

**Think About It:**

*Interest rates tend to fluctuate but also follow certain trends over longer periods of time. The 1970's and 1980's were generally periods of high interest rates. During the 1990's interest rates started to gradually decline approaching the lowest levels after the financial crisis of 2008/2009 (see chart below).*

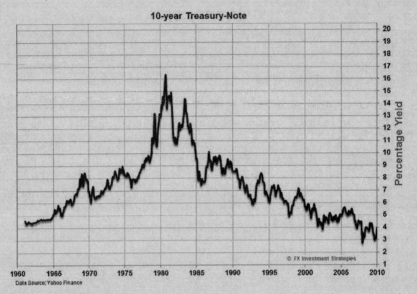

*It is conceivable that the trend will revert to higher rates within the next couple of decades. If interest rates were to rise substantially, this would leave particularly long-term bond investors with some price risk. Remember, longer maturity bonds are more prone to interest rate risk than short-term bonds. Plan ahead and do not invest your entire bond portfolio in long-term bonds.*

**Diversifying your Stock Allocation**

Although there are thousands of choices when it comes to selecting stocks, let's remember our previous discussion on the caveats of trying to outsmart the market by picking stocks. Instead of trying to pick individual stocks, it is better to spread the risk across companies and industries. As we learned earlier, an easy and cost effective way to do so is via low-cost index tracking funds. If you want to be as close as possible to the entire market performance, invest in an S&P 500 index fund. These types of index funds are a lot cheaper than your traditional mutual funds as we learned earlier. Over time, this can have a huge impact on the performance of your portfolio. Don't let your returns be diminished by paying additional fees!

## Rebalancing Your Allocation

As you get older, your allocation of bonds and stocks should change as well. At age 25, you would only have 25% invested in bonds. When you're 30 years old, make sure that 30% are now invested in fixed income investments. Most advisors will tell you that you should rebalance at least once a year. They do so primarily to accommodate age but also to adjust for changes in your personal life. The more active rebalancing strategies will include changes in the diversification among your stock holdings as well. But that approach would get a bit too technical for us here. Once you setup your low cost index fund to take care of your stock allocation, simply reduce the number of additional stock purchases and allocate more towards your bonds to rebalance the overall allocation to reflect your age in bonds.

◦◦

# Let's Recap...

Let's backtrack and recap our simple investment portfolio approach. Before considering any type of investment, we want to have at least one year's worth of living expenses saved up. Remember your **Essential Savings Goal** which is your safety cushion and is not to be touched other than for emergencies or when your income dries up.

Once you have reached your essential savings goal, you can then consider setting up an investment portfolio. I proposed the John Bogle approach of an age-based asset allocation wherein your age should determine the percentage of bonds or fixed-income holdings in your portfolio. The remainder should be placed in a low-cost index tracking fund. As you get older, the proportion of your fixed-income holdings increases. We also discussed the need to invest for the long-term and invest in regular intervals so that you don't buy all of your investments at the worst time. A consistent approach to long-term investing is as critical as a consistent approach to saving, budgeting and financial planning overall. Also, remember that there is no way to avoid risk completely. No pain, no gain.

So here we are now and you might ask, is that all there is to investing? No, of course not. This is just an example of a simple investment portfolio, your baby steps towards a life-time of investing. But for a start, this type of portfolio, properly setup and re-balanced about once a year, should provide you with an essential foundation that remains the core of your investment activities.

## Adding Some Spice To Your Portfolio

My basic advice to average investors in terms of picking specific assets or individual stocks goes something like this:

Unless you have a particular knowledge, insight or firm conviction about the economic prospects of an industry or a specific company, you are generally better off matching the overall market performance rather than trying to out-perform by picking individual stocks. The same could be said for other investments in all types of assets. That said, some folks feel that there must be something they can do to enhance their investment portfolio. Granted, they may also have some insight into certain trends you could capitalize on. Fair enough.

There are many ways to spice up your portfolio somewhat. For instance, you could consider investing in gold, silver or other precious metals. You could also take advantage of trends in alternative energy by investing in some alternative energy companies, solar energy firms come to mind. Again, diversification may be a good way to go here. Rather than trying to pick one particular company, invest in a fund that tracks the performance of a specific industry or commodity. For instance, rather than buying physical gold or silver, you could invest in an ETF that tracks the performance of these precious metals. But no matter what you invest in, consider these important factors:

- Learn everything there is to know about the asset and the proposed investment. The more you know about a particular industry, company or commodity, the better your chances to assess the risks. Remember that individual stocks and individual investments are more risky than an entire market/sector index.

- Limit the total amount of your investment escapades to no more than 10% of your entire investment portfolio. Any single investment in an individual stock or say one specific asset should not be more than 5% of your portfolio, preferably less. While any single investment could potentially outperform the major averages or your entire investment portfolio as a whole, it also bears much greater risk. When you take on greater risk with a specific investment, balance that risk against your entire portfolio.

## What About Property Investments?

Owning a home is at the center of the American dream. We all strive toward that goal in a way. For the vast majority of people, purchasing a home is the single biggest purchase they will make in their lifetime. There are many reasons why you would want to own a home. Some people view it as a long-term investment that may be sold during retirement. Other people view it as more of a family base, a true home for the family and something their children might inherit one day.

During the housing boom of the early 21$^{st}$ century, the notion of owning a home has turned into a greed driven race for money either through "flipping houses" or by extracting additional equity by refinancing mortgages. The notion that house prices could never come down and that there is no way to lose money by investing in property was obviously a flawed one. You know how the story ended.

Here's my take on this: Real estate can be a great investment if you know what you are doing. Buying a home can be a great way to build wealth over a long time frame, say, 30 years. Despite your investment considerations, owning a home also gives a sense of belonging and stability, potentially a home base for you, your family and future generations. But that huge investment does not come without risks and there are many costs associated with owning a home including the cost of financing the purchase. Remember our discussion about leverage earlier. If you don't have a sizeable down payment, the leverage of your mortgage can be devastating. I would only recommend a home purchase if you can come up with that down payment while leaving your essential savings goal intact.

ॐ

## Market Timing – The Grand Illusion

*"I can't recall ever once having seen the name of a market timer on Forbes' annual list of the richest people in the world. If it were truly possible to predict corrections, you'd think somebody would have made billions by doing it." - Peter Lynch, legendary investor.*

Wouldn't it be nice if one could figure out exactly when to buy and when to sell a company? That's wishful thinking according to another legendary investor, Warren Buffett. Instead, Mr. Buffet would tell you that it is impossible to time the market. In an interview in 2008 he said:

*"Most investors are better off putting their money in low-cost index funds and if they do it over time so that they don't buy it all at the wrong time, that's probably the best investment most people could make."*

Against this backdrop of wisdom, you may have heard some other statements prominently endorsed by the thousands of mutual funds out there. The most common tag line of mutual funds goes something like this: "If you had invested $10,000 in the year 19XX, you could have made $YYYY by now."

In reality though, nobody invests all his/her money in one stock or in one mutual fund and keeps it there for the rest of his/her life. Most investors buy some stocks and sell some stocks now and then. But rather than trying to do the impossible and time the markets, spread your investments over time.

Some people use a method called dollar-cost averaging. The idea is to buy a certain dollar amount of stocks at regular intervals, say every month, or 3-4 times a year depending on your preference. By committing a specified dollar amount you can average down your purchase price during periods of market drops by getting more shares for the same amount of money. This method has its advantages but you should keep in mind that transaction costs and commissions do put a bit of a dent in your performance. If you only trade a couple of times a year, it won't matter. However, if you were to trade each month those fees can make a difference.

You can also observe periods when the markets are in steep decline. Shortly after those periods are typically the best buying opportunities, again, if you factor in the longer time frame.

Over a 20 or 30 year time horizon however, the timing of your purchases becomes insignificant. What matters much more is your asset allocation and diversification. Over time, these two approaches bear more fruit than any stock picker or market timer with average investing skills could ever hope to achieve.

⁓

## What About Insurance?

Technically, I cannot give a professional opinion on the financial merits or the caveats of insurances. The insurance industry is a clearly defined subset of the financial services industry with its own rules and regulations. In a way, insurance agents are the step-brothers of stock brokers. Whereas brokers feed on people's greed, insurance agents feed on people's fears. In both cases it pays to take an objective look at the pros and cons and do your homework before signing on the dotted line.

Living without insurance is quite risky and it makes sense to protect your health and your most important assets. Here is a basic overview of the main insurance policies.

## Health Insurance
Your health is essential and in addition to eating healthy and exercising, carrying decent health insurance is helping you stay healthy. Remember that no matter how great your career might be, all the fame and fortune is meaningless if you're not healthy. Health insurance costs have been rising and will continue to do so in the foreseeable future, despite well-meant attempts by politicians to make health-care more affordable. It is therefore critical that you educate yourself on the pros and cons of different insurance plans and carefully consider all your options. Insurance is all about protecting your assets. Your health is your greatest asset. Make sure it stays protected.

## Car Insurance
If you live in cities like Los Angeles, a car is an essential part of managing your daily life. You have to protect your car against loss and damage. Also, consider a slightly higher coverage if you regularly keep some of your professional equipment in your car. If anything gets stolen from the car, you should be able to get a large part of the value of your equipment back.

## Property/Renters Insurance
A relatively inexpensive way to protect your personal property is through renter's insurance which usually covers all your personal property inside your apartment. The keyword here is "inside" the apartment. If your gear gets stolen anywhere else, it will not be covered. You can mitigate some of that risk with your car insurance as long as it has enough coverage for property left inside the car. But check to verify that your renter's insurance allows you to cover your professional equipment under their standard policies.

## Insuring Your Professional Equipment
You can insure your equipment separately but that doesn't come cheap. If you are a member of a union, or a music and arts organization, you can get discounts at certain insurance providers. Nevertheless, you need to assess whether your equipment is worth the price of insuring against theft. Some of your high quality instruments may well be worth it. However, some generic electronic equipment may not be worth the price. Remember my example about price depreciation earlier.

## Liability Insurance
You can add additional coverage to car and property insurance with a generic umbrella insurance which also protects against other personal

liabilities. Musicians and artists are typically not high profile targets for law suits but they can occur once you are making the big bucks. Like anything else, use a common sense approach to assess whether you have a high probability to get sued as a result of your (art)work or projects.

### Life Insurance

As long as you are young and without dependents (family, kids), life insurance makes no sense. In certain circumstances, a good life insurance policy may make sense for some individuals, for instance if they have special needs children who may require financial support during their adult life. Personally, I have a conceptual problem with generating a pay out when a death occurs. Even though I have a family with two kids, I don't have any life insurance. I feel that my money is better invested in an educational fund for my kids.

To summarize, the cost of insuring and protecting your assets can be quite high. As a general rule, read the fine print and really understand what you are protecting and what isn't covered. On a brighter note, some of the essential insurance policies like health insurance and car insurance are tax deductible when you are self-employed running your own business. This leads us to our next subject...

෴

## What About Taxes?

Tax planning is important in terms of achieving your financial goals. Remember it's not what you make but how much you can keep that gets you financially ahead. Taxes will put a dent on your net earnings no matter what. Unfortunately no one can avoid taxes completely.

Taxes and tax rules also seem to be getting more complicated each year and sadly, we won't have enough time to go over taxes in any detail in this book. In terms of your investment options, we can however look at some basic scenarios. Let's go back to our discussion of setting up an investment portfolio that works for you.

If you were a day trader and suppose you were profitable, almost all of your profits would be subject to short-term capital gains tax, which is set for holdings of less than one year. Although the tax law changes all the time, short-term capital gains tax rates are typically higher than those for long-term capital gains. By simply investing for the longer term, you're already in better shape than someone who's trying to chase short-term gains.

Another impact on taxes comes from your selection of mutual funds versus an index tracking fund. Mutual funds are essentially stock-picking funds. As each fund manager tries to outdo the market and the other fund managers, they have to pick new stocks and sell some other stocks from their holdings. The turnover from buying new stocks and selling old ones is much higher than the average index tracker. In essence, mutual funds are more exposed to short-term capital gains taxes which makes index tracking funds generally more tax efficient by contrast.

When you use an age-based asset allocation there is one additional tax advantage assuming you invested primarily in U.S. Treasuries. As you get older, the percentage of bonds in your portfolio increases. Gradually, your interest income from these bonds increases as well. Interest income is generally taxable but interest income from Treasuries is exempt from state and local income taxes.

There are of course many other tax implications depending on your personal financial situation. When you get ready to invest, keep in mind that taxes will be levied on your financial transactions one way or another. When the time comes and you're ready to invest, do some extra homework and learn more about optimizing your portfolio for taxes.

$\infty$

## What About Retirement Plans?

Most people associate a retirement plan with the so-called 401(k) plan. Named after the internal revenue code section 401(k), this type of retirement plan is setup by companies to provide some form of retirement benefits to their employees. A so-called 403(b) is the equivalent retirement plan offered by public schools and certain tax-exempt organizations. These plans offer some great advantages because employers can match part or all of your contributions to the plan. From a tax perspective, these plans are attractive because contributions to the plan can grow on a tax deferred basis.

In plain English, the amount you contribute to the plan each year can be deducted from your taxable income of that year, up to a certain limit. There are different types of 401(k) plans each with different rules and contribution limits. These contribution limits change as do the tax rules, so it's important to always keep up with the latest rules. Anyone employed by a company, school or non-profit organization should consider taking advantage of these types of plans, especially when employers match the contributions.

# Retirement Plans for the Self-Employed

This may surprise many of you, but you don't need to be employed by a company to setup a retirement plan or a retirement account. There are a number of options with different benefits and contribution limits.

### The Traditional IRA
The basic retirement account that anyone can set up, irrespective of employment status, is a traditional IRA (Individual Retirement Account). A traditional IRA is a basic retirement account that allows you to save and invest for your retirement. The contributions made to the IRA are tax deductible in your current tax year. Your contributions and any earnings from the investments in the IRA are tax-deferred. Eventually, you will have to pay taxes on the contributions as well as the earnings when you take out money during retirement. For the years 2010 and 2011 you could contribute up to $5,000 per year or up to 100% of your earned income, whichever is less.

Once you made your contributions it gets more difficult to pull money out of the IRA and for good reason. The IRA is meant for retirement. If you make any withdrawals from your IRA before the age of 59½ you will have to pay taxes and penalties. Not recommended! There are exceptions to this rule. You can make withdrawals without penalties for first-time home purchases ($10,000 lifetime limit), education, certain medical expenses and a few others.

IRA's are about as easy to setup as a bank account. You can open an IRA at banks and brokerage firms.

### The Roth IRA
A Roth IRA has many of the same features of a traditional IRA. Contribution limits are usually the same as well. There is one fundamental difference though. Contributions to a Roth IRA can only be made with "after-tax dollars," they are not tax-deductible. However, the big plus is that any earnings and all of the contributions to the account can be withdrawn free of taxes during retirement.

Another advantage of a Roth IRA is the ability to withdraw contributions at any time without taxes or penalties. If you were to withdraw interest or earnings like dividends, those of course would incur penalties. There some income limitations as to who can setup and contribute to an IRA, which is about $100,000 per year for a single person. But that's not something we should worry about as we start out becoming more financially independent. When the time comes and you make significantly more than $100,000, there are other retirement plans out there.

## What Is Better, Traditional Or Roth IRA?

The question boils down to this choice: Does it make more sense to take advantage of a tax break right now or enjoy tax-free withdrawals once you reach retirement? Contributions to a traditional IRA are tax deductible in your current tax year but you will have to pay taxes on your contributions and any earnings once you take out money during retirement.

A Roth IRA has no immediate tax benefits; contributions are made with after-tax dollars. However, those contributions and any earnings can grow tax-free and withdrawals can be made tax-free during retirement. You have to pay taxes one way or another, but you can choose to pay now or pay later. If you can't decide, you could open both retirement accounts. Put $2,500 in your traditional IRA and $2,500 into your Roth IRA to get a taste of both.

## SEP IRA's

Suppose you are starting to make more money and wish to contribute more towards your retirement. The traditional and Roth IRAs don't give you much room on the upside. But there is a good alternative especially if your income starts to go up as your career progresses.

The **S**implified **E**mployee **P**ension **I**ndividual **R**etirement **A**ccount better known as a SEP IRA can take care of that. This retirement plan is specifically designed for small business owners and self-employed individuals. You don't need to have your own company.
You can setup this plan as long as you do business in your own name for instance as an independent artist, graphic designer, composer, etc.

A SEP IRA works very similar to a traditional IRA in that contributions are tax deductible and earnings grow tax-deferred. Both contributions and earnings are not taxed until you withdraw them during retirement.

The big difference though, contribution limits can be a lot higher, which is a great benefit when you earn more income in one year and need higher tax deductions. If you were self-employed during 2010, you were able to contribute 20% of your compensation or $49,000, whichever is less. Say you were really doing well and made more than $100,000 in one year. When the time comes, you may need to find ways to lower your tax burden. With a traditional IRA, you are stuck with the maximum contribution of $5,000 per year. However, with a SEP IRA you could contribute up to $20,000 in that year.

There are income limits for SEP IRAs. But when the time comes and you make more than $250,000 per year, you should be able to hire a both a financial planner and a tax accountant who can then create the perfect financial plan for you.

SEP IRAs can be opened as easy as your traditional IRA. Most banks and brokers should be able to get you up and running within just a few minutes. SEP IRAs are also easy to administer in that there are no annual government reports or other admin burdens for you. If you have a business with employees, you can use SEP IRAs as the retirement plan for your employees. Those are still much easier to setup than 401(k)'s but you should get some professional advice before you consider setting up a retirement plan for employees.

Here's one more advantage of SEP IRAs which works particularly well for the self-employed with fluctuating income levels. You can setup a SEP IRA as late as April 15 for the previous calendar year. That also means you don't have to make any contributions until April 15 which is a great cash flow and planning advantage. In case you generate less business in one year, you are not required to make any contributions at all. You can skip contributions in any given year.

### Other Retirement Plans
There are other variations of IRAs and more complex retirement plans which may or may not be more suitable for your specific situation. The three plans we examined are the most popular and easiest to setup. Keogh Plans for instance are more complex and require a lot more administrative work. It's best to directly consult an accountant for something like that.

### Investment Options For Retirement Accounts
In terms of your investment choices, Traditional IRA, Roth IRA and SEP IRA are very similar to a regular brokerage account. That means you can essentially buy any type of stock, bond, CD, mutual fund or ETF. There are some limitations on Options and more complex investments – with good reason. These are retirement accounts and you should not take unnecessary risks with your retirement money.

**Keep in mind that the rules governing retirement plans as well as taxes are about as permanent as the fashion industry. They keep changing and evolving. Our brief tour through the world of taxes and retirement planning gives you just a generic overview and cannot cover all the bases.**

Before you get ready to setup your retirement account, you should find out more details specific to your personal financial situation. Hard to believe but the IRS website actually has lots of useful information about the different retirement plans.

You can also get any type of tax information at: **www.irs.gov**

Better yet, get some professional advice. Most brokerage firms have retirement specialists who can walk you through the different types of plans and help you setup your retirement account.

෬෧

## Final Words

Congratulations, you made it through the book! Hopefully this was a useful read giving you some good insights into the world of finance. Some of the concepts we discussed here may not have sunk in just yet which is perfectly normal. Nobody expects you to grasp all these concepts and become financially literate in a few weeks. In fact, I would highly recommend going over some of the book sections several times. Use this book as a general guideline, sort of your financial handbook. Whenever you run into a dead-end with money matters, this book is a good place to start in terms of providing some answers. But of course, the journey does not end here. There are thousands of books devoted to the world of finance. As we said in the beginning, this book is not one of those "Get Rich In 5 Weeks" kind of deals. This is a book about reality.

Think about your own career and consider how many years of studying and practicing it took to arrive at your skill level and knowledge. You don't just wake up one day to become a great writer nor do you learn how to play an instrument by just reading one book.

The path towards financial competence is not an easy one either. It takes a lot of effort, discipline and consistency to learn how to deal with your money. But if you follow the path we have started here, you should be well on your way to become more financially savvy and learn how to live well within your means.

**Best of luck with your finances and your career!**

# RESOURCES

## Money Music 101 Resources

Blog:                          www.moneymusic101.com

Resources & Calculators:       www.moneymusic101.com Click on "Resources"

## Recommended Websites

Yahoo! Finance:                www.finance.yahoo.com

Marketplace Money:             www.marketplace.publicradio.org/show/money

Get Rich Slowly:               www.getrichslowly.org

NEFE:                          www.nefe.org

Smart About Money:             www.smartaboutmoney.org

Investopedia:                  www.investopedia.com

Money Chimp:                   www.moneychimp.com

Jane Bryant Quinn:             www.janebryantquinn.com

Financial Times:               www.ft.com

FINRA:                         www.finra.org/Investors

Federal Reserve:               www.federalreserve.gov

My Money                       www.mymoney.gov

US Treasury:                   www.treasury.gov

Treasury Direct:               www.treasurydirect.gov

Tax.com:                       www.tax.com

IRS:                           www.irs.gov

## *Tools & Calculators*

Credit Card Payments:     www.federalreserve.gov/creditcardcalculator

FINRA Tools & Calculators: www.finra.org/Investors/ToolsCalculators/

Moneychimp Calculators: www.moneychimp.com/calculator

Mortgage Calculator:     www.mortgagecalculator.org

Investopedia:            www.investopedia.com/calculator


## *Recommended Books*

**Getting Things Done** by David Allen
Penguin (Non-Classics); (December 31, 2002)

**Making the Most of Your Money Now** by Jane Bryant Quinn
Simon & Schuster; revised edition (December 29, 2009)

**Your Money: The Missing Manual** by J.D. Roth
O'Reilly Media; 1st edition (March 2010)

**The Millionaire Next Door** by Thomas Stanley and William Danko
Taylor Trade Publishing; reissue edition (November 16, 2010)

**The 9 Steps to Financial Freedom** by Suze Orman
Three Rivers Press; 3 Rev Upd edition (August 15, 2006)

**The Little Book of Common Sense Investing** by John C. Bogle
Wiley; first edition. Illustrated edition (March 5, 2007)

**Economics in One Lesson** by Henry Hazlitt
Three Rivers Press (December 14, 1988)

**The World Is Flat** by Thomas L. Friedman
Farrar, Straus and Giroux; first edition (January 1, 2005)

**Investment Biker** by Jim Rogers
Random House Trade Paperbacks (April 8, 2003)

**The Only Three Questions That Count** by Ken Fisher
Wiley; reprint edition (October 20, 2008)

9463477R0011

Made in the USA
Charleston, SC
14 September 2011